Frederic Masson, J. M. Howell

Napoleon, Lover and Husband

Fre

de

ric Masson, J. M. Howell

Napoleon, Lover and Husband

ISBN/EAN: 9783337350512

Printed in Europe, USA, Canada, Australia, Japan

Cover: Foto ©ninafisch / pixelio.de

More available books at **www.hansebooks.com**

NAPOLEON,

LOVER AND HUSBAND

BY

FRÉDÉRIC MASSON

TRANSLATED FROM THE FRENCH BY
J. M. HOWELL

NEW YORK
THE MERRIAM COMPANY
67 FIFTH AVENUE.

COPYRIGHT, 1894,
BY
THE MERRIAM COMPANY

CONTENTS.

CHAPTER	PAGE
I. Youth	5
II. Thoughts of Marriage	19
III. Josephine de Beauharnais	32
IV. Citizeness Bonaparte	45
V. Madame Fourès	61
VI. Reconciliation	74
VII. La Grassini	87
VIII. Footlight Beauties	101
IX. Readers	116
X. Josephine's Coronation	131
XI. Madame * * * *	144
XII. Stéphanie de Beauharnais	157
XIII. Eléonore	171
XIV. Hortense	181
XV. Madame Walewska	192
XVI. The Divorce	237
XVII. Marie-Louise	252
XVIII. Elba	280
XIX. The Hundred Days	298
XX. Summary	310

LIST OF ILLUSTRATIONS

Bonaparte	Frontispiece
Josephine	Facing Page 32
Napoleon	" " 116
Hortense	" " 181
Marie Louise	" " 252

NAPOLEON, LOVER AND HUSBAND.

CHAPTER I.

YOUTH.

"PARIS, *Thursday*, 22d, 1787,
"Hotel de Cherbourg,
"Rue du Four-Saint-Honoré.

"AFTER leaving the Opera I wandered about in the garden of the Palais-Royal. Strongly impressed by the scenes which I had just witnessed, my mind in ebullition, exhilarated by the music, I was at first insensible of the cold; but, as the scenes which I had beheld faded, I became conscious of the wintry air and turned to seek shelter under the colonnade. I was upon the threshold of the iron gates when my glance fell upon a woman, and I stopped to look at her. The hour, her extreme youth, and general appearance left no doubt as to her social status, yet she looked modest, and when she stopped and confronted me it was not boldly but in a manner perfectly in accord with her appearance. Her diffidence encouraged me and I spoke to her; I, who have always been so impressed with the odiousness of such a calling as hers, have always shunned such women and considered myself contaminated by so much as a look from one of her class, now voluntarily addressed one; but this girl's pale face, delicate appearance, and sweet voice effaced all my old prejudices, and I said to myself: 'Here is a person whom it would be wise to study, as I desire to know something of this class of women.'

"'You look cold,' I said to her. 'How can you wander about on such a chilly night?'

"'The cold exhilarates me, and then—it is my life; I must seek acquaintances.'

"The indifferent and business-like tone of her answer pleased me, and I walked on beside her. 'You look delicate,' I said. 'I don't understand how you can endure such a life as yours must be.'

"'*Dame!* I must do something. I know no other way of earning a livelihood and I don't wish to starve!'

"'But could you not find some other occupation—something less wearing physically?' I asked.

"'Not now, it is too late.'

"I was delighted with her frankness, never having elicited such replies in my previous experiences.

'You must come from the North,' I said, 'since you do not mind the cold.'

"'Yes, I come from Nantes, in Brittany.'

"'I know that part of the country well. Mademoiselle, I wish you would tell me the story of your downfall.'

"'It was an officer, like yourself, who caused it.'

"'Do you regret it?'

"'I do indeed!' she answered, in a voice whose depth of feeling surprised me. 'I assure you I do; my sister is happily settled, and you cannot imagine how I wish that I too had a home.'

"'How did you happen to come to Paris?'

"'I was abandoned by the officer who seduced me and obliged to flee from my mother's anger; having made the acquaintance of another officer I accompanied him to Paris; then, he too left me, and a third, with whom I have lived for three years, succeeded him; although a Frenchman he was called by business to London and is still there, so I am obliged to shift for myself. Let us go to your rooms.'

"'Why should we go there?"

"'Don't be a silly! We will warm ourselves and then—perhaps you will be glad to have me there.'

"I was far from scrupulous and had piqued her

only that she should not run away from the sermon I was mentally preparing, and the modesty I intended to parade—before proving to her that it was a virtue I did not possess."

* * * * * * * * * *

At the time when this was written Bonaparte was aged eighteen years and three months, having been born on the 15th of August, 1769. We have the right to suppose that this was the first woman with whom he had any connection, and reviewing rapidly the history of his youth we shall find sufficient reasons to confirm this opinion. Napoleon himself made a note, with dates, of such love-affairs as left an impression upon his memory; those which I have been able to investigate I have found to be absolutely correct.

He left Ajaccio for France on the 15th of December, 1778, when he was but nine and a half years of age. The feminine memories which he carried with him from his island were those of his nurse, Camilla Carbone, who was the widow Ilari, and of a little schoolmate, "La Giacominetta," of whom he often spoke in the sad days at Saint Helena. Later in life he showered benefits upon his nurse, her daughter, Mme. Tavera, and her granddaughter, Mme. Poli, whom he had himself christened Faustina; he was unable to do anything for his foster-brother,

Ignatio Ilari, because when very young Ilari had espoused the cause of the English party and enlisted in the English navy.

Of the nurses who had charge of Napoleon's infancy and childhood one, Minana Saveria, remained until her death with Mme. Bonaparte; the other, Mammuccia Caterina, died before the Empire was established, as did also little Giacominetta, for whose sake, when a lad, Bonaparte had borne much teasing.

At the college of Autun, where he was a pupil from the 1st of January to the 12th of May, 1779; at the college of Brienne, where he was from May, 1779, to October 14th, 1784, at the military school in Paris where he spent the year from October 22d, 1784, to October 30th, 1785, no woman entered his life. Even admitting the statement advanced by Mme. D'Abrantès that, contrary to the strict rules of the Ecole Militaire, Bonaparte, under the pretext of a sprain, spent eight days in the apartment of M. Permon, No. 5 Place Conti, I see no reason to change my belief, for at that time he was but a stripling of sixteen.

Napoleon went to Valence on the 30th of October, 1785, and left that place to pass his vacation in Corsica on the 16th of September, 1786, after a sojourn of less than a year; he did not return from the island until the 12th of September, 1787, and it was then that he made his journey to the capital; therefore an adventure, prior to that of the 22d of November, 1787, could hardly have taken place between his leaving the Ecole Militaire and his return to Paris.

He did not engage in any gallantries while in Corsica, nor yet in Valence; indeed, during his sojourn in the latter place he appeared to be timid, rather melancholy, absorbed in his studies and desirous only of standing well in his classes and being well received socially. He had carried to Valence a letter of introduction to Mgr. de Tardivon, Abbé de Saint-Ruff, from the Marbeufs, and to this ecclesiastical dignitary, who, crossed and mitred, gave tone to the town, he owed his *entrée* into the best houses of the city, to Mme. Grégoire du Colombier's, Mme. Lauberie de Saint Germain's and Mme. de Laurencin's.

These ladies, particularly the latter two, held the best positions in the province, belonged to the lesser nobility and lived handsomely. They were prejudiced against the lives of the officers whom they admitted to their houses, and never permitted any intimacy between their daughters and young men whose conduct they did not consider irreproachable.

Bonaparte may have entertained some vague

ideas of marriage with Caroline du Colombier, who was permitted by her mother rather more liberty than other girls enjoyed. He was barely seventeen at that time, and she was considerably his senior; if he admired her, the attentions which he paid her were chaste, deferential and boyish: à la Rousseau. It was not long, however, before Mlle. du Colombier married an officer, M. Garempel de Bressieux, and left Valence and went to live in an old château in the country.

Nearly twenty years later, when Napoleon was in camp at Boulogne, he received a letter from her recommending her brother to his notice, and although he had not seen the object of his boyish admiration since her marriage, he answered by return of post, assuring her that he would seize the first occasion to be useful to M. du Colombier and saying:

"The memory of your mother and yourself has always been dear to me. I see by your letter that you live near Lyons, and I must reproach you for not calling while I was there, as it would have given me great pleasure to have seen you."

This advice was not lost, and when, on April 12th, 1806, Napoleon passed through Lyons on his way to the coronation at Milan, Mme. de Bressieux was among the first to request an interview. She was terribly changed, aged, and no longer the pretty Caroline of bygone days, nevertheless she obtained all she asked for : the erasure of certain names on the list of *émigrés*, a position for her husband, and a lieutenancy for her brother. On New Year's day of 1807 Mme. de Bressieux recalled herself to the Emperor's memory by a letter asking for news of his health. Napoleon responded promptly, and in 1808 he made her lady-in-waiting upon *Madame Mère*, called her husband to preside over the electoral college of Isière, and in 1810 created him a baron of the Empire.

Such was the grateful memory Napoleon cherished for all who had been kind to him in his youth ; there were none whose fortunes he did not assure, as there were none whom he forgot to mention during his captivity ; women, if possible, received the greater share of his gratitude, and even when he had reason to feel some bitterness towards them it was enough that they should once have shown him kindness. Thus Mlle. de Lauberie de Saint-Germain, like Mlle. du Colombier, had preferred another to him and married her cousin, M. Bachasson de Montalivet ; but Napoleon harbored no resentment, and it is well known that he made M. de Montalivet's fortune, creating him successively préfet de la Manche and of Seine-et-Oise, director general for bridges and public roads, minister of the Interior and count of the Empire with an endowment of eighty thousand francs. Mme. de Montalivet, of whom he once said, "Of old I loved both her virtues and her beauty," he named a lady of the Empress's household in 1806.

Mme. de Montalivet, however, did not accept this honor unconditionally, saying to the Emperor: "Your Majesty knows my belief regarding a woman's duty in this world; the favor which you have had the goodness to accord me, and which many will envy, would seem to me a misfortune if it prevented me from attending my husband when he has the gout, or nursing my children when Providence gives me any."

The Emperor at first frowned at Mme. de Montalivet's frankness, but after a moment said graciously: "Ah, madame, you wish to dictate terms; I am unaccustomed to that, but on this occasion I submit. Accept the position, and all shall be so arranged that your duties as wife and mother shall not be interfered with."

Mme. de Montalivet's position remained a nominal one, but that did not prevent Napoleon from showing her particular attention; he was fond of the whole family and said of them: "The family integrity is indubitable; it is composed of lovable people and

I believe firmly in the disinterestedness of their affection."

Such were the recollections which Napoleon had of Valence. They were dear to his heart, and of a kind which those young girls might well be proud of inspiring. He had no other intimacies that we know of, and in his private journal no others are mentioned; like Hippolite, he appears to have been more in love with glory in those days, than with women; in confirmation of this witness this extract from a letter written at that time:

"If I had to compare the days of Sparta and Rome with our modern times I would say *here* reigns love, *there* reigned love of country. Judging by the opposite effects which these passions produce one seems authorized in believing them incomparable. One thing is certain: people who abandon themselves to gallantry lose the ability to even conceive of the existence of a patriot, and we have reached that point to-day."

It is almost with a sense of certitude that we conclude that the girl he met in the Palais-Royal was his first mistress. The adventure, vulgar though it was, does not the less reveal his character; there is his misogyny, his critical spirit, brusque speech, and the habit of interrogation which he never renounced; his good memory, also, is noticeable in his account of it, for he reproduced in striking fashion the girl's manner of speech, even to the exclamation, *Dame!* which proved her Breton origin.

It is doubtful if Napoleon ever saw this girl again, for although among his papers, dated during that sojourn in Paris, there is a dissertation on patriotism which is addressed to a young lady, it is hardly a topic upon which one would write to a woman of her class.

After this sojourn in Paris, which lasted from October to December of 1787, Bonaparte again returned to Corsica, where he arrived on the 1st of January, 1788. He spent six months on the island, rejoining his regiment at Auxonne on the 1st of June; no trace of any love-affair at that place remains to us.

In the early part of 1789 he was sent to Seurre with a detachment, and is accredited with holding relations there, first with a Mme. L——z, *née* N——s, the wife of the collector at the salt depot, later with a farmer's wife, Mme. G——t, to whose house he went to drink milk, and, lastly, with the daughter of the house wherein he lodged. This seems crowding a good deal into twenty-five days, during which time his books are silent witnesses to his assiduous study; nevertheless, when, fourteen years later, on the 6th of April, 1805, Napoleon passed through Seurre on his way to Milan, it is claimed that M. de Thiard, who was at that time his chamberlain, introduced into his presence the boarding-house young woman, and that he presented her with a scholarship in a government school for her son, a lad of twelve. The stated age of this child precludes the idea that Napoleon believed him to be his son; moreover, had the Emperor entertained the least doubt upon the subject he would have done far more for the boy, and that without its being asked of him.

In Corsica, where he spent the entire year of 1790, at Auxonne, at Valence, again in Corsica, then, in the middle of 1792, at Paris, there were no love-affairs; we hear of none during the first campaign in the South against the Federalists, of none at Toulon.

We must deliberately skip over a period of four years, during which the young lieutenant became a general of brigade and was placed in command of the artillery in Italy, where, in 1794, the Convention sent one of its influential members, the Citizen Louis Turreau, on a mission to the army.

Representative Turreau was accompanied on his journey by his bride, who was the daughter of a surgeon at Versailles and a remarkably pretty woman; he arrived at Cairo, in Piedmont, where

Bonaparte was stationed, on the 21st of September, and, finding the young officer congenial, cultivated his acquaintance; while Mme. Turreau and the artillery-man soon arrived at an understanding, Bonaparte's intimacy with Mme. Turreau never assumed the proportions of a *liaison*, for she was too fickle to remain long constant, and, evidently, it never aroused the husband's jealousy, for he retained a high opinion of the young officer's ability, and when the Convention was in danger it was he, as well as Barras, who urged confiding the command of the troops to Bonaparte and, with the Corsican deputies, became his surety.

Bonaparte did not forget this service, and when placed in command of the army in Italy he took Turreau, who had not been re-elected, with him as commissary-general. Mme. Turreau again accompanied her husband, and, in default of the general-in-chief, made the best of such lovers as courted her; her conduct gave rise to continual scenes of jealousy, and Turreau, so it is said, died of a broken heart. The widow returned to Versailles, and in the early days of the Empire was dragging out a dreary existence there, when, one day, the Emperor chanced to mention her before Berthier, who was also a native of the town. The general had known Mme. Turreau from childhood, but for years had carefully shunned her; however, when he saw that the Emperor took an interest in his old schoolfellow, he renewed the acquaintanceship and espoused her cause, while Napoleon, never forgetful of a kindness, made haste to extricate madame from her financial embarrassment, granted all her requests and assured for her the realization of her rosiest dreams.

With the exception of Mme. Turreau, who threw herself at his head, women paid but scant attention to the little, pale, thin officer who was always badly dressed and regardless of his appearance, and Napoleon's early loves resolved themselves into trivial flirtations or vulgar adventures. He himself thought but little about women, being absorbed by his ambitious projects, and there was another, and valid reason for his chastity, he was poor. Poverty, however, did for him what it has done for many another man—forced him to consider matrimony that he might be the sole recipient of a woman's caresses.

CHAPTER II.

THOUGHTS OF MARRIAGE.

WHILE at Marseilles Napoleon played at love with Mme. Joseph Bonaparte's sister, Désirée-Eugénie Clary, then a pretty girl of sixteen; she believed his attentions to be serious. Her girlishness vanished and she developed a woman's affection for him. Sixty-five years later the rough drafts of her letters to Napoleon were found among her effects; they were all signed "Eugénie," for after the fashion of the time the young girl, whom her family called Désirée, had wished to be called by her lover by a name not used by others; these letters, which are the spontaneous outpouring of a pure affection, breathe the spirit of the period following upon the Reign of Terror, when women made love a religion; indeed, it was the only religion which existed on the ruins of society.

"Oh, my friend," Mlle. Clary wrote in one of her letters, "take care of yourself for my sake, for I could not live without you; guard as sacredly as I shall the promise which binds us, for were it broken I should die."

Napoleon's acquaintance with Mlle. Clary dated from January or February, 1795, and the engagement, if there was a formal one, must have taken place on the 21st of April, when Bonaparte passed through Marseilles on his way to Paris. There was no opposition to the marriage from the Clary family, for Joseph and his wife had long desired it, and Désirée's father, who is reported to have said "that one Bonaparte in the family was quite enough for him," had died on the 20th of January, 1794, and the remaining members of the family, Mme. Clary and her son, readily yielded to the young girl's wishes; her youth was no obstacle to the marriage, for at that time girls were usually wed in their eighteenth year, and the First Civil Code had just fixed the thirteenth year as the legal age for a female to marry. Désirée Clary afterwards claimed, and officially stated, that at this time she was between thirteen and fourteen years of age, but she must have been nearer seventeen, as she was born on the 9th of November, 1777.

Bonaparte arrived in Paris in May; he was out of favor, out of funds, and his only hope lay in this marriage, failing in which nothing remained for him but to take service in Turkey, or, like many others, to speculate in national securities. Even when, by degrees, his position improved, and he was employed by the Committee on Public Welfare on plans for the campaign, his position was precarious, and realizing its instability, believing that his sole salvation lay in this marriage, he urged Joseph to have a date fixed for the wedding, and in every letter which he wrote his brother at that time messages for Désirée appeared.

For a while Mlle. Clary was a faithful correspondent, but while at Genoa with her sister and brother-in-law she neglected her lover, and in one of Napoleon's letters he said, "The road to Genoa leads through the waters of Lethe," called her the "silent one," and constantly reproached her for not writing. Finally, becoming impatient, he determined that a definite understanding should be arrived at, and wrote to Joseph that he *must* interview Désirée's brother and bring the matter to a head, and the following day, without giving his first letter time to reach Joseph, he wrote again saying: "This affair must either be concluded or broken off. I await an answer with the greatest impatience." Then a month passed, and save for friendly messages there was no correspondence between the pair.

The truth is, that Paris, the unknown, fascinating

city which he had entered with a worn uniform, leaky boots, and a suite composed of a couple of hungry aides-de-camps had interposed itself and its captivating women between Napoleon and the little Marseillaise. What a contrast there must have been between the immature girl and the elegant and worldly women of the capital! Désirée could hardly have been beautiful, though there must have been a certain charm about her soft eyes with their penciled brows, *retroussé* nose, laughing mouth and reserved yet tender manner; but between the young provincial and the elegant, graceful, well-dressed and beautiful, if artificial, Parisian women, there was the same difference as lies between hothouse fruit and that which ripens in the open air. The Parisians, created for a life of gaiety and excitement, highly refined in manner and adepts in the art of pleasing, were like hothouse fruit, which, carefully tended, reaches the highest state of perfection, and when exhibited to the best advantage by the fruiterer appears, with its fine color and bloom, which the winds of heaven have never visited too roughly, much more appetizing than the fruit of the orchard which, kissed by the sun, whipped by the breeze, and not quite ripe, leaves in the mouth a fresh but somewhat tart taste.

"In Paris alone," wrote Napoleon, "live women

capable of holding the helm. A woman should live six months in Paris to learn what is her just due, and where her rightful domain." A few days later he wrote: "The women here, who are certainly the most beautiful in the world, play a great rôle in all the affairs in life."

The women who figured conspicuously in the society of that day certainly were beautiful and possessed of even a greater charm, a perfect knowledge of the amenities of life; better versed in the art of inspiring affection than able to give it, they completely fascinated the young officer, and, having nothing save his hand to offer, he proffered that freely, laying his heart and hand first at the feet of Mme. de Permon, then proposing to Mme. de la Bouchardie, later to Mme. de Lesparda and finally to Mme. de Beauharnais who took him at his word.

During all this time he never wrote to Désirée, and at last she lifted her voice in complaint, but so gently, so sweetly, that it sounds in one's ears like the sad strains of an Æolian harp. "You have broken my heart," she wrote him, "yet I am weak enough to forgive you everything. You are married and I have no longer the right to love and think of you; the only consolation which remains for me is to be assured of your belief in my constancy, then I long for death, for life is a burden, now that

I may not consecrate it to you. I cannot accustom myself to the thought that you are married—it is too hard, too cruel! I will prove to you that I am more faithful to my engagement than you to yours, and, though you have broken the chain which united us, I shall hold it binding; I shall never marry. I wish you every happiness and all prosperity in your marriage, and I hope that the woman you have chosen will make you as happy as I had meant to do, and as you deserve; but in the midst of your happiness remember poor Eugénie and pity her sad fate."

Forgetfulness was foreign to Bonaparte's nature, and the memory of this love which he had inspired was always a tender point with him; from a flirtation he had insensibly drifted into an entanglement which had ambition for its basis, and which had resulted in the breaking of a heart, and throughout his life he strove to undo the wrong and win forgiveness. While at Milan, in 1797, he planned a brilliant marriage for Désirée, who was in Rome with her sister and brother-in-law, Joseph being then ambassador at the court of Pius VI. and gave a warm letter of recommendation to General Duphot in which he spoke of him as "a fine man and distinguished officer;" and in a personal letter to Joseph he said, that an alliance with General

Duphot would be a desirable one. Duphot made a favorable impression upon Mlle. Clary, and their marriage contract was about to be signed when the terrible scene of December 28th took place and Désirée's dress was stained with the blood of her betrothed.

After refusing several offers, Désirée finally consented, while Napoleon was in Egypt, to marry General Bernadotte. It was considered a fine match, but he was a most insupportable Jacobite, narrow-minded and opinionated; a Bearnais by birth, he yet had none of the Gascon's sprightliness or readiness of speech, but possessed all their shrewdness and hid under apparent frankness a scheming brain. He held Mme. de Staël to be the cleverest of her sex because she was the most pedantic, and he spent the honeymoon in laying down the law to his young wife.

The news of this marriage reached Bonaparte at Cairo, and although Bernadotte was his enemy, and the union displeased him, he wrote most kindly to Désirée, wishing her all happiness.

When Napoleon returned from Egypt the first person to solicit a favor was Mme. Bernadotte, who asked him to stand godfather to her infant son. Intuitively she knew that a son was the one thing lacking to complete Napoleon's happiness, and, as if to spite Josephine, whom she hated, and whom she always spoke of as the "old woman," Désirée boasted of her maternity. Bonaparte kindly consented to stand for the child, and with Ossian's martial ballads in mind named the baby Oscar. Years later Napoleon said: "Bernadotte's becoming a marshal of France, prince of Pontecorvo and king of Sweden was all owing to his marriage with my first sweetheart," and it was for her sake that Napoleon pardoned all Bernadotte's disloyalty during the Empire.

From the very first Bernadotte manifested his opposition to Bonaparte; nevertheless, he was called to a seat in the Council of State, then named general-in-chief of the army in the West, where he not only opposed, but openly conspired against the First Consul, aspiring to gain command of the army. For this he received no punishment. Bonaparte simply, in order to get rid of him, appointed him minister plenipotentiary to the United States, a post which Bernadotte expressed himself as perfectly willing to accept, playing his game so well, however, that the frigate which was to bear him to his destination was never ready to sail.

The following year saw the conspiracy in which Moreau was implicated, and Bernadotte again escaped unpunished, because Napoleon so willed it, Désirée's welfare being always in his mind; he did still more for her, for, redeeming Moreau's estate, his property at Grosbois, and his hotel in the rue d'Anjou, for which he paid four hundred thousand francs, he presented it to Bernadotte. The Empire established, Napoleon, for Eugénie's sake, created her husband a marshal of the empire, chief of the eighth corps of the Legion of Honor, president of the electoral college of Vaucluse and *Chevalier de l'Aigle Noir;* for Désirée's sake he gave the couple an income of three hundred thousand francs, a lump sum of two hundred thousand francs and the sovereignty of the principality of Pontecorvo. For the love of her Napoleon forgave Bernadotte after Auerstaedt, Wagram, and Walcheren, condoned two military blunders, which were probably something more serious than blunders, coming as they did on top of a flagrant conspiracy in which Bernadotte, Fouché and Talleyrand, in complicity with the royalists, brought into play the same tactics by which, in 1814, the return of Louis le Désirée was effected.

Thus, over her husband's shoulders, Napoleon's one-time sweetheart received attentions and favors which would be surprising did we not know that he was ever actuated by the desire to atone for the sorrow and mortification he had once caused her. Two days after the battle of Spandau, in which Bernadotte was wounded, Napoleon wrote to him, saying:

"I am glad to learn that Mme. Bernadotte is with you; pray give her my affectionate regards and add that I have one little thing to reproach her with. She might have written me a line giving me the news of Paris, but I will have it out with her when we meet."

Although Mme. Bernadotte never appeared at court, for she detested Josephine and the entire Beauharnais family and was at no pains to conceal her dislike, Napoleon showered gifts upon her. He presented her with priceless Sèvres vases and Gobelin tapestries, it was for her that he reserved one of the three magnificent fur pelisses which the emperor of Russia presented to him after Erfurt; yet, appearances to the contrary, his friendship was entirely disinterested. Was it not of Désirée's aggrandizement that he was thinking, when, after Walcheren, he meditated sending Bernadotte to Rome as governor-general to represent the court of France at the Quirinal, thus creating him a high imperial dignitary with an emolument of three million francs, and putting him upon an equality with Borghèse who was at Turin, Elias at Florence, and almost with Eugène who was at Milan?

When the sovereignty of Sweden was offered to Eugène de Beauharnais he declined the honor, not wishing to become an apostate, and it was due to the good-natured neutrality of Napoleon that Bernadotte was elected hereditary prince of that country. If Napoleon's political moves at this period are incomprehensible to some historians, it is because they failed to take into account the part which his heart played in the affairs of state; he was seduced by the pleasure of seeing the woman in whom he took so warm an interest become a queen, his godson heir apparent to a throne. He regulated minutely the details of Désirée's presentation and leave-taking as princess of Sweden, and, unprecedented favor, he invited her to one of the family's Sunday dinners. He conferred upon the newly-elected prince of Sweden a purse of a million francs from the public treasury, repurchased the property with which he had originally presented him, negotiated with him the return of Pontecorvo and gave a title and sum of money to Bernadotte's brother; certainly Napoleon was justified in writing to Désirée, "You must long since have been convinced of the interest I take in your family."

Four months after the receipt of all this kindness Bernadotte combined with Russia against Napoleon; less than a year afterwards everything indicated that a rupture between France and Sweden was imminent, and Désirée, who had most reluctantly consented to take a short journey to Stockholm, then made haste to return to her hotel in the rue d'Anjou.

Then, exercising the greatest caution, Napoleon wrote to the minister of Foreign Affairs requesting that he speak to the Swedish ambassador regarding Désirée's presence in France, and state, as delicately as possible, that he was sorry to see that the Princess Royal had come into the country without permission, which was not customary, and that he regretted her leaving her husband under the existing circumstances. Désirée paid no attention to the ambassador's admonitions, but proceeded to install herself, and in November, when war was about to be declared, the Emperor wrote a second time and sent Cambacérès to the queen of Spain (Julie Clary) saying that he wished the princess to leave Paris and return to Sweden as it was not proper that she should be in France at that time.

His wishes availed nothing, and Désirée remained in Paris, continued to order her dresses from Leroy, to receive her friends and hold her receptions; she went to the baths with her sister and returned to Paris as though nothing unusual was taking place; she even considered it singular that the Frenchmen whom she received should blame the former marshal of the Empire who had then assumed command of the allied forces in the north of Germany. If one can believe those who claim to be well informed, Désirée was both ungrateful and a traitor, and while conveying to her husband Napoleon's adjurations, acted between Bernadotte, Fouché and Talleyrand as an intermediary.

If demonstrated that Désirée profited by the Emperor's weakness for her to become a link in an intrigue between conspirators who knew each other of old, one must think badly of her character, and it is pleasanter to believe that she remained in Paris because of her love for the city, that she might not leave her sister, nieces and friends, or be obliged to alter the habits of a lifetime.

She was in Paris in 1814, and took part, with other people of rank, in the visit of Alexander of Russia; she was still there in 1815, during the hundred days, and on the 17th of June, the eve of Waterloo, she ordered a nankin riding-habit and a percale dressing-gown trimmed with valenciennes from Leroy; her lack of interest in Napoleon's success in the stupendous game he was playing, with all Europe for his adversaries, clearly proves that hers was the forgetful spirit.

CHAPTER III.

JOSEPHINE DE BEAUHARNAIS.

Towards the end of October, 1795, hazard brought together the Vicomtesse de Beauharnais and General Bonaparte. The latter had sprung suddenly from obscurity to publicity, and his name, but recently so little known that Barras had written it "*Buona-Parta*," had been spoken in thunderous tones to the whole of France by the cannon which crushed the rebel sections of the Convention.

Second in command of the army of the Interior, soon to be commander-in-chief, Bonaparte had ordered the disarmament of the Parisians. A youth came to his quarters begging permission to keep his father's sword; Napoleon saw the boy and, being attracted by him, granted his request, and the mother then called to express her thanks. She was a great lady, a ci-devant vicomtesse, the widow of a president of the Constituency, of a courtier, of the commander-in-chief of the army of the Rhine, and she was a revelation to Bonaparte; her title, birth

JOSEPHINE.

and education, the easy, graceful manner in which she expressed her thanks, all charmed him. For the first time in his twenty-six years of life the young provincial, to whom no woman of quality had ever paid the slightest attention, found himself in the presence of one of those elegant, accomplished and desirable creatures whom he had seen and admired from afar. He was in a position which gratified his pride, that of a protector, and this rôle which he played for the first time suited him marvellously; while Mme. Beauharnais, who was reduced to all sorts of expediencies, discerned at once what manner of man she had to deal with.

A creole, native of the island of Martinique, she had been married at the age of sixteen to the Vicomte de Beauharnais; a marriage arranged by her aunt, who lived openly with the Marquis de Beauharnais, the bridegroom's father. From the time she first came to Paris, in 1779, Josephine Tascher de la Pagerie, Mme. de Beauharnais, led a wretched existence; deceived and abandoned by her husband, and finally separated from him, through no fault of hers, she had no social distractions; she was never presented at court, for she lived with her aunt whose position was equivocal, but it is claimed that after her separation from her husband she made use of her liberty. Returning to Martinique she remained there until her safety was threatened by the insurrection, when she escaped to France, and becoming reconciled with M. de Beauharnais, who was then deputy of the Etats-Généraux, president of the Constituency and general-in-chief of the army of the Rhine, she enjoyed a brief period of happiness; her salon was then frequented by men of note and letters, and for the first time she tasted the sweets of social position. Then came the Reign of Terror; Beauharnais was imprisoned and guillotined and she escaped only by a miracle.

When released from prison Josephine de Beauharnais was thirty years of age, the mother of two children and penniless. Aided by some feminine connections which she had formed in prison, for she had none elsewhere, she launched herself into society. With the money which she received from Martinique, loans which she made wherever possible, debts which she contracted in every direction, she managed to keep up an appearance. She left her apartment in the rue de l'Université and rented from Louise-Julie Carreau, the wife of Talma, for the sum of four thousand pounds a year in cash, or ten thousand in notes, a small hotel, No. 6, rue Chantereine, where she installed herself in October, 1794.

A year passed, debts accumulated, and nothing

came in ; probably with creole *insouciance* Josephine failed to give proper consideration to her financial affairs, or hoped that some miracle might extricate her from her difficulties, and, while showing herself everywhere where the society of that day amused itself, she picked up acquaintances who were instrumental in the restoration of some of her husband's property, but she ran through it as fast as it came into her possession. She possessed nothing, neither capital nor fixed income. At her marriage she had received a dot of one hundred thousand francs from which she was to receive a yearly interest at the rate of five per cent. ; but her father was dead, her mother very poor, and the island blockaded by the English. Her aunt, Mme. Renaudin, had given her some unimproved real estate, but it had long since been disposed of ; moreover, no one can squeeze an income out of unimproved property, and of credit she had none. Mme. Renaudin helped her a little by loans, and there were one or two obliging bankers who accepted drafts on Martinique, who even advised her going to Hamburg where she could receive her remittances with less trouble ; but she was in a desperate position, credit exhausted and age creeping on ; it was at this critical moment that General Bonaparte rang the bell of the house in the rue Chantereine and returned the visit of Mme. la Vicomtesse de Beauharnais.

Napoleon did not know that the house, which was rather imposing in appearance, was the property of Citizeness Talma, who, when she was Mlle. Julie, had received it as a price of her favors to a lover; nor did he know that this property, in an out-of-the-way corner of Paris, within a stone's-throw of the rue Saint-Lazare, on which its garden, in almost its original extent, touches to this day, was worth only fifty thousand francs. A man-servant responded to the bell and ushered the general through a long open passage, on one side of which, in a sort of pavilion, the stable was situated, its open door revealing two black horses and a red cow; the carriage-house, which contained a shabby carriage, was carefully closed.

The passage gave into a garden in the centre of which stood the house, a modest structure of one story and basement surmounted by a mansard; four high windows pierced its façade and a low porch, with a simple balustrade in the style of a terrace, ran across it. Bonaparte mounted the steps, entered an antechamber, scantily furnished by a brass fountain, the lower half of an oak wardrobe and a pine settee, from whence the servant introduced him into the dining-room, where he was free to choose between a seat on one of the four black haircloth-covered chairs which surrounded the mahogany table, or to wander about and look at the engravings which, framed in black and gold, decorated the walls. The room was not luxurious, but here and there serving tables, of mahogany or of the yellow wood of Guadaloupe with marble tops and gilded trimmings, bore witness to former opulence; while behind the glass doors of two cabinets a collection of table accessories, and a tea-service of English plate made a fine showing; of silver, in the proper sense of the word, there was none.

Josephine, all tricked out by her maid, the Citizeness Louise Compoint, hastened to the dining-room to greet her guest; she could not receive him elsewhere as the first floor of the house comprised only that apartment, her bed-chamber and a small apartment which served as a dressing-room.

Josephine's bedroom, though simple, was tasteful and pretty, the furniture was of mahogany and the yellow wood of Guadaloupe; there was a gay toilet set of blue nankin with decorations of red and yellow coxcombs, the low double bed was daintily draped, and the room was ornamented by a harp of Renaud's make and a little marble bust of Socrates; the dressing-room, with the exception of a Renaud piano, was chiefly furnished with looking glasses; there was one on the toilet-table, another on the chest of drawers, one on the night stand, and over the chimney hung a double pier-glass.

Such were the surroundings of this high-bred woman. Except on festive occasions, when she brought out a small service of blue and white porcelain, she ate off earthen-ware; the table linen was composed of eight tableclothes, of which four were of bird's-eye, and all so worn, that when the inventory was taken the entire supply of household linen was estimated at a value of four pounds. Bonaparte was ignorant of all this; he did not know that the elegant and charming woman who stood before him, whose tasteful toilet pleased his eye, whose infinite grace troubled his senses, possessed scarcely enough underwear to clothe her decently; he saw only a charming and elegant woman, a woman to arouse desire.

Josephine's hair was brown, of a fine quality but not over luxurious; however, in those days, blonde wigs and a suspicion of powder were in vogue; her complexion was rather dark and already somewhat faded, but art concealed the ravages of time; her teeth were poor, but were never displayed, and she had a dear little mouth which was always curved in a slight smile, the sweetness of which accorded with the exceeding softness of her eyes, with her gentle expression and the touching quality of her voice, to catch a sound of which the servants, in later years, loitered in the corridors of the Tuileries. Her nose was small, with sensitive, quivering nostrils, and slightly inclined to be *retroussé.*

Her head, however, was not to be compared with her tall, supple body, which terminated in slender, arched feet, whose beauty may yet be divined by a glance at the shoes she once wore. Her form was unfettered, she did not even wear a girdle to support the bosom, which was, however, very small. General effect is everything, and this woman possessed a charm and grace peculiarly her own ; long practice had rendered her every movement graceful and refined ; she never lost an advantage, was constantly on her guard, leaving nothing to chance, and she had that indefinable nonchalance of the creole which is so attractive, while about her floated like a perfume that sensuality which makes the creole woman essentially feminine and is so intoxicating to man. Napoleon, younger and more inexperienced than the majority of men, was peculiarly susceptible to it ; it was that about the woman which had appealed to him at their first meeting, even while she dazzled him by her imposing manner, which he spoke of as being "that calm and dignified demeanor which belongs to the old *régime.*"

Mme. de Beauharnais saw that the young officer was completely captivated, and when he called the following day, and the day after, and so on day after day, she understood that her empire over him was absolute. Seeing Mme. de Beauharnais surrounded by men of the old court who were his superiors by rank and birth, Ségur, Montesquiou, Caulaincourt, all of whom treated him with a certain degree of familiarity, Napoleon failed to perceive that these men, who, in his estimation, had lost nothing of their former prestige, came to her house as bachelors, to divine that their wives would not visit there. Coming from the Jacobin circle in which he had always lived, and which at Vaucluse, Toulon, Nice, and Paris had advanced his interest, he took infinite delight in the company in which he found himself. The luxuries of the lady, like her nobility and social position, were all delusions, but his senses aiding, were accepted by Napoleon as realities.

A fortnight after his first visit they were lovers. Judging from writings they were still only friends, but a witness of the times tells us that transitions were rapid, that fine distinctions were not made, and the world moved fast.

They loved passionately. Such love was natural enough on his part; on hers—well, possibly it was equally so, for Bonaparte was a new toy, a savage to be tamed, and the lion of the day.

To a woman like Josephine, no longer in her first youth, such ardor, such intense passion, burning kisses and constant craving for her presence, was the most flattering of tributes, for it proved that she was still beautiful and able to please. All this made Napoleon attractive as a lover, but hardly recommended him for a husband; however, when he offered himself, he was accepted, for she was in a desperate situation and had nothing to lose by the marriage, while it offered a chance of betterment. Bonaparte was young and ambitious, was general-in-chief of the army of the Interior, the Directory had not forgotten that it was he who arranged the plans for the last Italian campaign, and Carnot proposed creating him commander-in-chief in the approaching campaign; such a marriage, therefore, might be her salvation and committed her to nothing, for divorces were easily obtained in those days when there was no longer any question of priests and religious ceremonies, and it was simply a contract which endured as long as both parties desired to observe it, but which meant nothing either to the woman's conscience or to society.

Bonaparte was a man capable of great things, and Josephine argued that if she played her part well she would share any honors accruing to him, while if he was killed she was sure of a pension as his widow. Nevertheless, she took some precautions; in the first place she dissimulated about her age, for she did not wish either her young lover, or any one, to know that she had passed her thirty-second year. Accompanied by Calmelet, her confidential adviser and one of the guardians of her children, and by a person of the name of Lesourd, she went to a notary's where those two certified: "That Marie Josephine Tascher, widow of Citizen Beauharnais, was well known to them, that she was a native of the island of Martinique, and that as the island was at that moment occupied by the English it was impossible for her to secure a certificate of her birth;" armed with this legal document Josephine was able to declare to the civil officer that she was born on the 23d of June, 1767, whereas she was born on June 23d, 1763.

Josephine also deceived Napoleon regarding her fortune, which one would suppose was a difficult thing to accomplish, but Napoleon accepted all her statements, and there was drawn up privately, with only the general's aide-de-camp, Lemarrois, as witness, the strangest marriage contract which had ever come under the notary's observation. There was no property in common of any sort, complete authority was given by the prospective bridegroom to the prospective bride, the guardianship of her children by her first marriage remained entirely with her, and a dowry of fifteen hundred pounds of rent was bequeathed her in the event of his death, and in that event all property belonging to her previous to this marriage was to be restored.

Personal property there was none; all that the future wife possessed belonged to the estate of herself and the late M. de Beauharnais, and no inventory of it existed; it was therefore impossible for her to decide whether she would keep it for her personal use or share it with Bonaparte. Such an inventory was taken two years later and Josephine refused all claim to the property. In those two years she had bettered herself. Napoleon frankly avowed his lack of fortune, declaring himself possessed of no real estate and no worldly possessions other than his wardrobe and military equipments which were valued by him at a nominal sum suggested by the notary. He was really, as the notary said to Mme. de Beauharnais, "as poor as a church mouse." Bonaparte himself thought the declaration of his worldly possessions ridiculous, and simply erased that paragraph from the marriage contract.

The contract was dated March 8th, 1796, and the following day the marriage was celebrated by a civil officer, who was gracious enough to register the groom's age as twenty-eight, and the bride's as twenty-nine instead of thirty-three; Barras, Lemarrois (who was not then of age), Tallien and the inevitable Calmelet were the witnesses. There is no mention of the parents of either party having sanctioned the marriage, and probably they were not consulted.

Two days afterwards General Bonaparte left to join the army in Italy, while Mme. Bonaparte remained at her home in the rue Chantereine.

CHAPTER IV.

CITIZENESS BONAPARTE.

Napoleon was ten days on the road between Paris and Nice, and from every posthouse where he stopped for relays, he dispatched a letter to the "Citizeness Bonaparte, in care of Citizeness Beauharnais."

In these letters there is naught save love; ambition finds no place; there is no reference to his plans, no incertitude expressed regarding the future; he was so sure of himself, that he felt no need of a confidant, or of discussing his intentions and the likelihood of his success. He was like a prince of bygone days sallying forth to an assured victory, and his letters to his bride breathed only passionate love.

From the moment that he arrived at Nice, even while speaking a few brief words to the demoralized troops which constituted his army, words which encouraged their hopes and roused their enthusiasm, even while enforcing obedience from the revolting generals, while organizing, equipping and providing for the nourishment of the disorganized forces which he was to lead across the Alps, he found time to write letter after letter to Josephine. "When tempted to curse my fate," he wrote, "I lay my hand over my heart, and, feeling your picture there, love renders me supremely happy, and all of life seems bright, save the time which I must spend away from you." Napoleon never parted from the miniature to which he referred, showed it to every one and prayed to it at night, and when by accident the glass was broken, he was terribly distressed, fancying it presaged death.

Bonaparte's love for Josephine was like the adoration of the faithful, the exaltation of the believer; if the soldiers knew of his infatuation they did not make sport of it, for the majority were of his age and race, and extravagant dreams filled their brains as well as his.

In spite of his youth, Napoleon was just the man to lead such a strangely assorted army; his thin, pale, immobile face, framed by long locks, which he wore slightly powdered, impressed the soldiers by its inscrutability, his piercing eyes seemed to read their very souls, his glance cowed them. Below him in command, were such men as Augereau, a deserter from half the armies of Europe, a familiar old fellow and a bully, and Massena, one-time smuggler and pirate, as fond of women as he was of money, and indifferent to the means of securing both. These men would gladly have overthrown the young upstart who was in command of them, but he looked them straight in the eye, and, like wild beasts before the tamer, they growled, but grovelled. The mass of officers and soldiers, for there were not many such ruffians as Landrieux, did not need to be cowed, for their hearts were Napoleon's from the first; the greater part of the men had been in the Egyptian army and had served an apprenticeship of abnegation; each had in his soul something of the spirit of La Tour D'Auvergne, and was animated by patriotism and love of glory.

In this war, officers refused advancement as an insult, corporals turned the tide of battle, common soldiers improvised themselves into generals and devised strategic movements; an electric current of genius circulated in the ranks; men disdained death and were gay in the face of it with joyous stoicism. In all these respects Napoleon was a worthy commander; to vanquish, to conquer the enemies of France, were the means by which he would be enabled to see his beloved and have her at his side, and with this desire urging him on, he won, in April, 1796, six battles, took twenty-one flags and forced

Piedmont to capitulate. "My brave boys," he said to his troops, "I appreciate and am grateful for your gallant conduct!" and doubtless he was thoroughly sincere, for, thanks to their gallantry, Josephine could join him.

Napoleon despatched Junot to Paris with the hard-won trophies and with orders to bring Mme. Bonaparte back with him, and to his wife he had written, "Hasten, for I warn you that if you linger you will find me ill; fatigue and your absence combined are more than I can bear." It was no lie to draw her to his side, for he was consumed by a continual fever and exhausted by a persistent cough; the itch, from which he had suffered at Toulon, had reappeared and affected his stomach, making him almost consumptive, while his incessant craving for Josephine also wore upon his health. He wrote to her, "You are coming, are you not, my darling? You will soon be here at my side and I can hold you in my arms, close to my heart which beats only for you. Oh, take wings, beloved, and fly to me!"

No other woman had the least attraction for him. At Cairo, a prisoner of war, the mistress of a Piedmontese officer was brought to his tent; she was young and beautiful and at sight of her his eye gleamed for a moment, then he greeted the captive with calm and gentle dignity, and keeping his officers with him, arranged for her transportation to the outposts and return to her lover.

In this case he may possibly have been actuated by motives of policy, but at Milan, when Grassini made every effort to seduce him, singing for him so exquisitely that the whole army were enthralled, he paid the singer but repulsed the woman. There was only one woman in the world for him then, and the voluptuous happiness he found in her arms satisfied all his desires, he longed only for her caresses and was impatient for her arrival.

Following the fortunes of war was not to Josephine's taste; she found it far more agreeable to remain in Paris and enjoy the fruits of her husband's success, which had made her one of the most courted women of the capital, than to share his fortunes in camp. No one refused credit to the wife of the general-in-chief of the French forces in Italy; moreover, Bonaparte had sent her power of attorney, so that she was able to indulge her extravagant tastes; she was at every *fête* and ball, at all the receptions at the Luxembourg, which under Barras had recovered their princely splendor, and where, next to Mme. Tallien, who was the social leader, Josephine was the most important of the ladies.

She was the cynosure of all eyes when, after Junot had presented the Directory with the trophies of her husband's battles, she left the hall leaning on his arm, and she gloried in the adulation which her husband's victories had brought her. When she entered her box at the theatre the parquet rose as one man and cheered; at official *fêtes*, at the celebration of the victories, it almost seemed to Josephine that the honor was hers, so great was the attention paid her. Paris, too, enchained her; the city had taken such a hold on her that the idea of living elsewhere was intolerable, and ever afterwards that feeling predominated; she strove to the end of her days to remain in Paris.

Napoleon awaited her arrival in a state bordering on frenzy; he was both anxious and tormented by jealousy, and wrote letter after letter, sent courier after courier to hasten her coming. "What are you doing?" he wrote her, "why do you not come? If it is a lover that detains you, beware of Othello's dagger!"

Josephine found it necessary to invent excuses for her delay, as Joseph Bonaparte had been sent to hasten her departure, and Junot, in spite of the pleasure he took in exhibiting himself in his hussar uniform, was about to rejoin the army, so, unless she could hit upon a really good excuse for remaining in Paris, she knew she must accompany him. After Chérasco had followed Lodi, and the army was at that moment at Milan, therefore it was no longer a bivouac but a palace which awaited her.

Poor health was an old story, but an illness occasioned by the beginning of pregnancy she thought would be an excellent excuse, and, indeed, when that news reached Bonaparte he was delighted. In one of his letters he says to her, "I have wronged you greatly, and I do not know how I shall ever expiate my fault; I reproached you for remaining in Paris when you were suffering. Forgive me, darling, for the love with which you have inspired me has deprived me of my common sense; I shall never regain it; I am incurable. I am filled with gloomy forebodings; I fear for your safety; could I but hold you in my arms I should be happy; but the distance which separates us fills me with misgivings. A child, as adorable as yourself, will soon lie in your arms! . . . It seems to me that could I but see you once, hold you for an instant in my arms, I should be content, but, unfortunate man that I am, I cannot go to you even for a moment."

On that same day he wrote to Joseph:

"My friend, I am in despair, for my wife, the only creature in the world whom I love, is ill, and I am oppressed with the most gloomy forebodings because of her condition. I beseech you to tell me exactly how she is, and by the tie of blood and the tender friendship which unites us, beg that you will give her the tender care which it would be my greatest joy to give her. You cannot love her as I do, but you are the only person on earth who can, even in a measure, take my place; you are the only man on earth for whom I have always entertained a warm and constant affection, you and my Josephine are the only beings in whom I feel any interest. Reassure me; tell me the truth. You know my ardent nature, that I have never loved before, that Josephine is the first woman I have ever truly cared for, and you can understand that her illness drives me distracted. I am alone, given over to fears and ill health, nobody writes to me and I feel deserted by all, even by you. If my wife is able to stand the journey I desire that she should come to me, for I need her. I love her to distraction and I can no longer endure this separation. If she has ceased to love me my mission on earth is finished. I leave myself in your hands, my best of friends, and I beseech you to so arrange matters that my courier will not be obliged to remain in Paris more than six hours, to hasten his return with the news which will give me new life."

Napoleon had become really desperate and threatened, if his wife did not join him, to send in his resignation, abandon everything and return to

Paris. Josephine realized that further excuses were futile; she could not deceive Joseph by pretending illness, for he saw that she was able to go to every entertainment and bore the fatigues of pleasure remarkably well; while as for her last and best excuse, that which had touched her husband so deeply, it was too evidently a fiction for her to insist longer upon it. So at last she was obliged to prepare for the hated journey, and after a farewell supper at the Luxembourg, in the lowest of spirits, blinded by tears, she stepped into a travelling carriage and, in company with Joseph Bonaparte, Junot, Citizen Hippolyte Charles, the assistant of Adjutant-General Leclerc, her maid Louise Compoint and her dog Fortune, she started for Milan.

Louise Compoint, nicknamed the officious, ate at the same table with her mistress, was almost as well dressed, and had little of the menial about her. Her room in the rue Chantereine in nowise resembled a servant's, but with its curtains and portières of Siamese stuff, alabaster and gilt candelabrum, Sèvres statuettes and jardinières and handsome brass-trimmed furniture was really better appointed than Mme. Bonaparte's. Louise Compoint's relations to Josephine were doubtless those of a confidante whom it was desirable to conciliate, for, although they afterwards disagreed, she paid the girl a pension up to 1805. During the journey, which was slow and seems to have been designedly prolonged, Junot managed to ingratiate himself into Mlle. Louise's good graces, and although Josephine subsequently showed herself far from indifferent to the admiration of M. Charles, she was for the moment furious because Junot preferred her maid to herself.

Although the travellers left Paris at the end of June they had not reached Milan on the 8th of July, and Bonaparte, who was obliged to leave there and go to face Wurmser's army, sent a courier begging his wife to join him at Verona. "I need you," he wrote, "for I feel that I am on the eve of a severe illness." Josephine, however, preferred to await his return to Milan, whither he rushed the moment he could leave the field, and they spent two days together, then he was obliged to face the crisis at Castiglione.

Never was there a graver situation, danger more imminent, it was not simply a question of avoiding defeat, but of annihilation; yet during the terrible mental strain which followed, when he was massing his divisions and manœuvring to prevent disaster, at the moment when his destiny was at stake and his star seemed to waver, when, for the first time, he was assailed with doubts of himself, Napoleon still found time for a daily love-letter. "Show me some of your faults," he wrote, "be less beautiful, less gracious, tender and good, above all never be jealous and never weep, for your tears drive me crazy, they fire my blood. . . . Rejoin me as soon as you possibly can, that ere death can part us we may have more happy days together."

Throughout their entire separation the same wild passion was daily expressed ; in order that Josephine should rejoin him, so that he might sometimes spend a day or an hour in her society, he entreated, implored, and finally was forced to command ; and she, grown a little more submissive in the face of conquered Italy and that fantastic army, feeling vaguely that her husband belonged to the race of chiefs whom one must obey, made the effort to join him.

It was a strange journey which Josephine made across a country torn by war ; sometimes she was forced to flee before the Austrian forces, sometimes she made a triumphal passage through the towns of new Italy, where she was welcomed like a sovereign ; it was made through armies sometimes victorious, sometimes disbanded ; she travelled in carriages, which were continually being upset, and on horseback ; and in the brief intervals of her perilous journey Bonaparte made ardent love within the sound of drums beating a charge, under fire, and by the light of bombarded cities.

When Josephine was with him Bonaparte spent the entire time at her side in an attitude of devotion; when absent, he sent courier after courier bearing messages of affection; from every one of those unknown towns, whose names he rendered immortal, he dispatched letters in which passionate declarations of tenderness, of confidence and even of gratitude are mingled with jealous imprecations. It was a constant cry from a hungry heart, from a man who had lived chastely, towards the mistress older, more worldly, more sophisticated than himself, who satisfied his heart and senses.

Unintentionally, Bonaparte borrowed his epistolary style from Rousseau, not that he was insincere or that his love was a pretext for literary efforts, but because he was imbued with that style; he did not know, and never learned how to speak of love in any other fashion; he was a disciple of Jean-Jacques to the end of his days. Josephine was neither of the same nationality, education or temperament, and his perpetual elation and continuous demands upon her affection wearied and bored her. It was pleasant to hold the first place in the heart of so extraordinary a man, and his youthful fervor interested her at first, but there was a brutality in the expression of his love which shocked, rather than appealed to her jaded senses, and often rendered her husband's caresses repugnant.

She was recompensed in a measure for the unpleasant experiences of her sojourn in Italy by the offerings from cities, princes, generals and merchants which poured in upon her; but although she received and spent a great deal of money, she was not a mercenary woman. As prodigal as shortsighted, easily tempted and yielding, Josephine accepted willingly and gave capriciously, seeing no wrong in either course, and simply obeying her instincts; nevertheless she managed that Bonaparte remained in ignorance of her doings, knowing that he entertained scruples which were incomprehensible to her. Among the first presents offered her in Italy was a box of rare medals, à *propos* of which Bonaparte had so strongly expressed his disapproval that she had felt obliged to return them; after that experience she took good care to keep him in ignorance, and whenever he questioned her as to how jewels, valuable pictures and priceless antiquities came into her possession she accounted for them by clever inventions, in which proceeding she was ably seconded by her accomplices.

There were many things of which Bonaparte was ignorant, among them the existence of General

Leclerc's assistant, M. Charles, who had remained in Milan, and paraded the streets, foppishly arrayed in a cavalry uniform, invariably appearing at the Palace Serbelloni during its master's absence. M. Charles was a well-built, active young man, gay, witty and possessed of the most imperturbable assurance. Josephine claimed that their friendship was purely platonic, that the young man was merely a pleasant companion who helped her to while away the time, but it is certain that he was also the go-between between the creole, who was always in need of something, and the shopkeepers who fancied that the general's wife could be useful to them, and he was a lavish contractor, levying gaily upon whatever was needed with the jolly inconsequence of a soldier foraging.

Bonaparte finally became suspicious of M. Charles, as he had of Murat, and upon some pretext the young man was arrested; upon his release he left the army and returned to Paris, where Josephine secured him a position with the Compagnie Bodin, and he made a large fortune in the provision business.

M. Charles had been a companion to Josephine's taste, some one from her beloved Paris, gay, noisy, amusing Paris which she missed so much, and she needed some one of his calibre to help her bear the intolerable *ennui* to which she was a victim. "I am bored to death," she wrote her aunt, and indeed she was; she was bored by the demonstrative affection of her young husband, bored at Milan and Genoa where she was received like a queen, bored at Florence where the Grand Duke welcomed her as "My Cousin," at Montebello where she held her court, at Passeriano and Venice, bored everywhere outside of Paris, yet, when Bonaparte finally turned his face homeward, she did not accompany him; she had taken a fancy, so she said, to see Rome, and she did not reach the rue Chantereine until her husband had been a week settled in the house whereon, at her orders, one hundred and twenty-five thousand francs had been expended in furniture and decorations.

Thus, for a caprice, Josephine renounced the triumphant journey across Switzerland and Italy, during which Bonaparte was everywhere greeted with shouts of acclamation, the victorious return to France by the side of the man with whose praises the whole country was ringing, the man whose glorified name she bore.

Although at that time Napoleon's ardor had somewhat abated, his wife was still the only woman whom he loved, and he made a public confession of his affection, saying to Mme. de Staël, "I adore my wife," he never left her, and was not displeased by the report that he was extremely jealous. Josephine was no longer pretty, she was nearing forty, and showed her age, but in Bonaparte's sight she had not changed, and, his first passion passed, there remained so sweet and tender a memory of his first love that throughout his life she exercised over his heart and senses an immutable influence.

NOTE.

A chronicler, whom I only cite because in such matters it is wisest to take note of all that is said, affirms that on the morning when Bonaparte received the oaths of the civic guard, he had in his apartment an actress, who was a mistress of a Piedmontese general, and whom he had ordered brought there for his amusement, and that, the ceremony terminated, he went on foot to the *Passage des Figini*, where he purchased from Manini the jeweller, feminine ornaments valued at a hundred and twenty-eight pounds. Another account, that previous to the taking of Milan he had for a mistress the Marquise de Bianchi, a woman of remarkable beauty, who had called upon him to reclaim twenty-five horses belonging to her husband which the French had stolen. After the marquise he is accredited with having entertained an opera singer named Ricardi, to whom he presented a carriage and six horses; after that, a youthful dancer of seventeen, Mademoiselle Thérèse Campini, and, lastly, the daughter of a furrier. That makes five, and none of the adventures, and I have carefully investigated the subject, appear to be authentic.

CHAPTER V.

MADAME FOURÈS.

BONAPARTE stood on the deck of the transport l'Ocean as she sailed out of the harbor of Toulon on the 29th of April, 1798, and watched Josephine until distance hid her from his sight. He still loved her fondly, if not with the burning ardor of the first days of their married life, and admired her as the incarnation of grace and elegance, of all that was sweet and feminine, and as the first woman who had been completely his own and rendered him supremely happy.

It had been settled between them that as soon as Egypt was conquered (and he did not doubt that he should conquer) he should send a frigate for her and she should join him, in the meanwhile she was to go to the baths; but if Josephine was sincere when she promised to go to Egypt, the idea of making such a journey, of going into an unknown land, soon became a bugbear to her, the old Parisian life reconquered her, society and the world resumed their sway, the attachment she had formed at Milan was hard to break, and she lingered in France.

Reports of her indiscretions reaching Napoleon on the passage between Malta and Alexandria, his old suspicions were awakened, and he felt he must know the truth; so he called aside those whom he judged to be his sincerest friends and least likely to deceive him, and, determined to learn what had been said of his wife in Italy, pressed them with questions. Men were blunt in those days and he was soon fully informed.

Josephine's life before he married her did not interest him and he asked no questions about it. When he had written her from Milan: "Everything pleases me, even your errors and the trying scene which preceded our marriage by about a fortnight," he gave the keynote to his character and explained his comprehension of love. In his opinion the right a man has over his wife dated from the day they are wed, and from the day when Josephine de Beauharnais had bound herself to him by an oath, accepted his love and professed to share it, she belonged wholly to him; if she had deceived him he was done with her.

The idea of divorce germinated in the hour when his eyes were unsealed and the illusion under which he had lived was dispelled. Had Bonaparte remained in ignorance of Josephine's infidelities he would doubtless have been as faithful in Egypt as he was in Italy, but under the circumstances he felt under no obligation to restrain himself, and saw no reason why he should not lighten the tedium of the hours by the distractions, which, a few months previous, would have seemed to him like treachery to his wife, but which under the existing conditions appeared but natural to a man of his years.

He had a fancy to taste of the far-famed charms of Oriental women, as so many other Europeans had done, and a number were introduced to him, but their obesity was repugnant, for no one was ever more easily disgusted, more sensible to odors, or more impressionable than Bonaparte.

He was more fortunate at the Egyptian Tivoli, a garden constructed on the model of the Tivoli at Paris and managed by a member of the old body-guard, once a schoolmate of Bonaparte's at Brienne, who had obtained permission to follow the army. Like its prototype, the Egyptian Tivoli had a club with all kinds of games, swings, jugglers, snake-charmers and dancers, and its habitués could take an ice while listening to the strains of a military band. The place would have been pleasant if frequented by the feminine habitués of similar European resorts, but of European women there were few, the only ones who frequented the Tivoli having come with the army to Egypt; for, in spite of the order that officer's wives were to remain behind, a few, disguised in male attire, managed to evade the scrutiny of the sentinels and make the passage in the holds of the transports; they were mostly bold, audacious creatures, old campaigners accustomed to a life of adventure, and, like the wife of General Verdier, able to handle a gun as well as their husband.

The prettiest among these women was a little blonde with dazzling complexion and white teeth, by name, Marguerite-Pauline Bellisle. She would have been attractive anywhere; in Egypt she was simply adorable. Apprenticed to a milliner at Carcassonne, she had succeeded in marrying her employer's nephew, Lieutenant Fourès, a good-looking young fellow in the 22d chasseurs. In the midst of their honeymoon came the order to embark for Egypt; the bride arrayed herself in cavalry uniform and sneaked aboard the same vessel which carried the groom; arrived at Cairo she resumed her feminine habiliments and devoted herself so exclusively to her husband that the union was cited as a model one.

During a fête, given at Esbekieh after a review of the troops, Bonaparte's young aides-de-camps, Merlin and Eugène de Beauharnais, caught sight of Mme. Fourès and admired her so vehemently that his attention was directed to her, and he inquired who she was; that evening he saw her again at the Tivoli, was introduced and paid her marked attention. Afterwards, intermediaries, who are to be found everywhere, undertook to smooth the way for him.

Whether from calculation or virtue, it was some time before the little woman yielded; it required protestations, letters and rich gifts to overcome her scruples, but at last she succumbed. On the 17th of December Lieutenant Fourès received an order to embark, alone this time, on the Chasseur commanded by Captain Laurens, with orders to make the coast of Italy and carry dispatches to the Directory; at Paris he was to see Lucien and Joseph Bonaparte, and, after receiving such letters as they desired to send, to return to Damiette. He returned sooner than was expected.

The day after the lieutenant's departure Bonaparte gave a dinner at which Mme. Fourès occupied the seat of honor. The host was most attentive, but towards the end of the repast, with apparent awkwardness he upset a carafe of ice-water over her, and rising, with many apologies, led the way into another room, under pretext of assisting her to rearrange her disordered toilet. A chronicler of the times tells us that "they paid some regard to appearances, but unfortunately their absence was so prolonged that the guests who remained at table entertained grave doubts as to the genuineness of the accident." They had still more cause for doubt when a house adjoining the palace Elfi-Bey, the general's residence, was hastily furnished, and the fair Marguerite stalled therein.

Madame Fourès was scarcely settled in her new abode when her husband returned. The Chasseur sailed from France on the 18th of December, and the following day fell a prisoner to the English man-of-war Lion; the English, who were pretty accurately informed regarding what was going on in the French army, were malicious enough to send Fourès back to Cairo on his parole not to serve against them during the war. The lieutenant, who Marmont vainly essayed to detain at Alexandria, arrived in a furious temper, and cruelly did his wife expiate her faithlessness; to escape his rage she petitioned for a divorce, which was pronounced by a military justice, and on the return of the Syrian expedition Lieutenant Fourès was again ordered to return to France, and an express order to expedite his journey was addressed to the naval commander.

After her divorce, Mme. Fourès, who had resumed

her maiden name of Bellisle, paraded herself as Bonaparte's favorite. Richly apparelled, living in most luxurious fashion, entertaining generals and doing the honors of the palace to some army women, she was to be seen everywhere; sometimes driving with Bonaparte, while the aide-de-camp on duty trotted by the side of the carriage—Eugène de Beauharnais like the rest,—sometimes galloping about in a general's uniform, a cocked hat perched on her head, and mounted on an Arab horse which had been especially broken for her use. "Here comes our general!" said the soldiers, while those addicted to flowery language nicknamed her, "Cleopatra."

About her neck she habitually wore a long chain to which hung her lover's miniature; it was a public *liaison* at which no one manifested any astonishment.

From the year 1792 young women in masculine apparel were to be found at all the headquarters of the Army of the Republic, sometimes acting as aides-de-camp, as did the demoiselles de Fernig, but more frequently in another capacity, like Illyrine de Morency, Ida Saint-Elme and many others. At that epoch a man's costume was to be found in the wardrobe of every woman of easy morals, the generals' custom of taking their mistresses, and even their wives, on military expeditions was so deep-rooted that during the campaigns in Spain, and up to the fall of the Empire, hardly one failed to follow it; for example, witness Massena in 1810 and 1811. Nevertheless Eugène de Beauharnais rebelled against his duties as escort to his stepfather's mistress, and was excused from that service, though he was still retained as aide-de-camp.

So deeply enamored was Bonaparte of Marguerite Bellisle, that he did not conceal from her his intention of repudiating Josephine; and even meditated marrying her should she bear him a child, but as he laughingly remarked: "The little idiot does not know enough to have a baby," which being repeated to her drew forth the retort: "Who knows if I am the idiot?"

During the Syrian expedition Marguerite remained at Cairo, and Bonaparte wrote her the tenderest letters, and when, after Aboukir, the general embarked on the Murion to return to France, he left orders that the ci-devant Mme. Fourès was to rejoin him as soon as possible, and that she should sail by the first armed vessel.

General Kléber, however, did not take that view of the situation. He had succeeded Bonaparte in command, and doubtless he regarded La Bellilote as one of the perquisites of the position; at all events he threw obstacle after obstacle in the way of her departure, and it was owing to Desgenettes that she finally embarked on a neutral vessel, the America, in company with Junot and some of the savants of the Egyptian expedition, Rigel, Lallemand and Corancez, Jr. Unfortunately the America fell into the hands of the English, and Mme. Fourès was not released from captivity and able to return to France until too late.

When she reached her native land the reconciliation between Bonaparte and Josephine was an accomplished fact, and her lover metamorphosed into the First Consul of the Republic, a position which rendered it incumbent upon him to set the country an example of a dignified and upright life. It is claimed that Bonaparte forbade Mme. Fourès coming to Paris; if so, his injunctions were disregarded, for she came and showed herself in company with her friends at "Les Français" and other theatres; the Consul, however, firmly refused to see her, but gave her as much money as she demanded. On the 11th of March, 1811, he presented her with sixty thousand francs out of the appropriation for theatres, he bought a château for her in the suburbs of Paris, and arranged a marriage between her and M. Henri de Ranchoup, an émigré, an ex-infantry officer, and the scion of a good Auvergne family; the marriage took place at Belleville in 1800, and the husband received as a wedding-present the vice-consulship of Santander, from which he was promoted, in 1810, to the consulate of Gothenburg.

In spite of her husband's duties, Mme. de Ranchoup appears to have been seldom absent from Paris; she was there in 1811, and still there in 1813. In 1814 she was well known in society and visited the Baroness Girard, the Countess de Lucy, and the Baroness Brayer; she went in for literary work, and had published by Delaunay a two-volumed novel entitled "Lord Wentworth." The romance of her life, however, is far more interesting. She painted also, and was not without talent if one can judge by the charming portrait she made of herself, wherein she appears pulling the leaves from a daisy; it was a singular idea to thus represent herself essaying to read her fate by the aid of a flower. Alas, for her! while searching for "passionately" she found "not at all." The portrait represents a charming woman with a vivacious face under a mass of short, babyish curls, slight, graceful figure and really beautiful arms, and it atones in gracefulness for what it lacks in technique.

Towards 1816 Mme. de Ranchoup came to an open rupture with her husband, sold her furniture, which was valuable, and departed for Brazil in company with an ex-officer of the Guard, Jean-Auguste Bellard. It was rumored in Paris that, having realized on her property, she proposed to renew her relations with Napoleon and aid him to escape from St. Helena. She was not thinking of such a thing, having grown to detest the Emperor, and to affect royalistic opinions. When Mme. d'Abrantès published her memoirs she mentioned this rumor, praising Mme. de Ranchoup highly for her loyalty and devotion; but the latter protested, as such a statement rendered her a suspicious character in the eye of the police, who, knowing her to be an old friend of Bonaparte's, were inclined to keep an eye upon her and who watched her narrowly when she returned from Brazil with Bellard in 1825.

In reality her journeys between Brazil and France were taken simply to secure to herself a competency; she took out merchandise, which she exchanged for rosewood and mahogany, these she brought back and sold in France, returning again to South America with furniture; oscillating in this fashion between the Old World and the New until 1837, when she settled in Paris. She continued writing, and published another novel, "Une Châtelaine du XII. Siècle," and installed in a modest little apartment in the rue de la Ville-l'Evêque, surrounded by monkeys and birds, she led a cheerful, contented existence until the 18th of March, 1869, when she died at the age of 92 years. She retained all her faculties unimpaired to the last; she wrote, played on the harp, and painted; she bought pictures, kept up her friendships with the women she had known in other days and even made new friends, among others, Mlle. Rosa Bonheur.

Mme. de Ranchoup's taste in art is discerned by the numerous pictures with which she endowed the museum at Blois (to which city she was attracted by her friend the Baroness de Wimpffen). Many of these pictures which claim to be Raphael's, Titian's, Léonard's, and Boucher's, are really only copies; some canvases are attributed to Prud'hon, others to Reynolds, Terburg, Jean Meel, Carlo Maratti, Jeaurat, and there are also two modern pictures, one a Rosa Bonheur, the other a Compte-Calix; infant Jesus', Bohemians, Venuses, Cupids, Psyches and Hermits, abound; but not one recalls the days in Egypt, the palace of Elfi-Bey, and the man who played the most important rôle in her life. Before she died, Mme. de Ranchoup, or the Countess de Ranchoup, as she preferred to be called, burnt every letter which had been written her by Bonaparte. It appears as though she wished to annihilate every memory of the love to which she owes her place in history; that youthful, sensual love which had, nevertheless, an ingenuous side, and in which, above all, we see how imperious was Napoleon's desire for a child; a child of his own, to whom he could transmit his name and his glory.

CHAPTER VI.

RECONCILIATION.

JOSEPHINE was dining at the Luxemburg, a guest of Gohier, president of the Directory, when the news that Bonaparte had landed at Fréjus was announced : it was totally unexpected and almost overwhelmed her, for she had well-nigh forgotten that he existed, had seemingly overlooked the possibility of his return, and arranged her life to please herself, her conduct closely resembling that of a widow no longer inconsolable.

While in Egypt the husband meditated a divorce, in France the wife was making her repudiation imperative ; having broken off her relations with Barras, whose influence was declining and whose power was weakening, she did everything to ingratiate herself with the Gohiers, husband and wife, from the moment he held an important government position.

Gohier was a native of Rennes, belonged to the middle-class, and had been the minister of Justice during the Reign of Terror ; he it was who drew up the legal formulas which Fouquier-Tinville enforced ; he was the casuiste of the guillotine. Nothing gives an air of austerity like the hunt after judicial expediencies, it is the indispensable mask which hides the law's prevarications, and Gohier affected a Spartan-like integrity and sternness.

Because of his austerity he was elected a member of the Directory, and because of it also he made a recruit of Josephine, who confided to him her passion for M. Charles, and was counselled by him to apply for a divorce in order to espouse her lover.

Josephine, though tempted, hesitated ; but in the meantime, because of M. Charles, she quarrelled with her brothers-in-law, Joseph and Lucien, who were the most violent adversaries of the Gohier party, and inspired their life-long enmity.

On the Bonaparte side were all Napoleon's friends, those who waited, hoped and counted upon his return to re-organize France, while the Gohier party comprised his bitterest enemies, Bernadotte, Championnet, Jourdin, Moulin, all the political generals. The Jacobins had pushed forward Gohier, who was a republican and a civilian, solely that they might encompass the downfall of the conqueror. The more hostile Gohier was to Bonaparte, the better it suited Josephine, and, in order to secure to herself the protection and support of the Gohier family, she schemed to marry her daughter Hortense to their son ; planning to sacrifice the poor child (whose happiness was always a secondary consideration) if it proved to her interest to do so.

This scheme was progressing finely, and they were dining *en famille,* when the startling news that Bonaparte had disembarked and was on the way to Paris came upon them like a thunderbolt.

It was clear that he would not have come in so secret and unheralded a fashion save for grave reasons ; Gohier realized that a crisis was at hand, and Josephine that she had not a moment to lose if she would save herself, for, seeing a struggle for supremacy, she meant to be on the winning side. Gohier might yet be a useful friend, but the most important thing was to regain her empire over Bonaparte. With this end in view, she instantly determined to go to meet him, and announced that determination to Gohier. "Do not fear, President," she said, as she took leave of him, "that Bonaparte comes with designs fatal to liberty, but it is wiser to prevent traitors from gaining his ear."

She hurriedly ordered post-horses and set out; this time without Louise Compoint, or Fortuné ; and, unincumbered by baggage, flew to meet her husband. Her plan was to throw herself into his arms, rekindle his burnt-out passion, and win him back, and by thus avoiding all explanations return with him to Paris, and be at his side to receive the chagrined Bonapartes who would again hesitate to speak, or, if they dared, would find they spoke to deaf ears.

While Josephine was urging on her postilions, and eagerly scanning the horizon for the travelling-carriage she so wished to meet, Bonaparte arrived in Paris by the Bourbonnais route; learning this she hastily retraced her steps, but she had lost three days, during which Bonaparte had interrogated his brothers, sisters and mother, who confirmed the gossip he had heard in Egypt, and cemented his determination to obtain a divorce. There was no longer any doubt as to what Josephine's conduct had been in Milan, or of the life she had led during the past seventeen months. It seems that the Bonapartes, either out of regard for her or their brother, did not tell all they knew, possibly they did not know everything; however, what they said sufficed; Napoleon's decision was taken, and the whole family approved it.

In vain did the friends, to whom he recounted his troubles, remonstrate and point out to him that the acclamations with which the people had greeted his return proved that they looked to him for their salvation, that they did not expect a scandal, that he must wait until he had done his duty to his country before he dismissed his wife, that to advertise his domestic troubles was to lay himself open to ridicule, and that in France ridicule kills; to all Bonaparte turned a deaf ear.

"She must go," he said, "no matter what people say; they will gossip for a day or two, then all will be forgotten." No consideration could soften or touch him, no interests were great enough to overthrow his just indignation. To avoid a meeting wherein he feared he might be moved to pity—for he realized the hold Josephine had over his senses, and would not trust himself to meet her—he deposited with the concierge her jewels and effects; he then made an appointment with his brothers for the following morning, intending to settle the last formalities, and alone in his room on the first floor of the house, awaited their arrival.

Josephine, half frantic, at last reached the rue Chantereine; it was a desperate game she was about to play, and her chance of success was poor, for her cause was already half lost.

During her journey, for perhaps the first time in her life, Josephine had reflected upon her position and the horror of it had burst upon her, forcing her to see that if she did not succeed in seeing, and re-conquering her husband, she had nowhere to go. Men like M. Charles were well enough for a pastime, but how could she have been so stupid as to permit her relations with him to have become a scandal and for his sake to jeopardize her best interests? That, the affair with Barras and others, the Bonapartes antagonized, debts everywhere—what *was* to become of her? Her head was in a whirl. Not realizing the value of money, she had bought continually on credit, fancying that all her bills were settled when she had only paid something on account, and she dragged after her then, as she did during the Empire and up to her last hour, a train of creditors who always gave her fresh occasion for expense and whose bills she increased without a thought of the day of reckoning. When payment became due she wept and sobbed, lost her head, resorted to every possible expedient, called on God and the devil to help her, and, when she succeeded in gaining a little time, thought herself saved. This was how she stood at that moment; to her tradespeople alone, it is said, she owed twelve hundred thousand francs, and it is not unlikely, for that was the usual sum of her indebtedness. She had purchased in the canton of Glabbaix, in the department of Dyle, national bonds to the amount of one million, one hundred and ninety-five thousand francs, and still owed two-thirds on it; the other third was to have been furnished by her aunt, Mme. Renaudin, then become Mme. de Beauharnais, but she had not a penny and could not fulfill her promise. She had bought of citizen Lecoulteux the lands and demesne of Malmaison for two hundred and twenty-five thousand francs; thirty-seven thousand, five hundred and sixteen francs for furniture, utensils and provisions, and nine thousand, one hundred and ten francs for rights and privileges; on this she had paid for the furniture with "the price of diamonds and jewels belonging to her:" but the rest was demandable, and who was to pay it?

Josephine knew she might claim that the general, who had visited Malmaison before his departure for Egypt, had offered two hundred and fifty thousand francs for the property, and that that was about the sum which she had agreed to pay for it; but after having seen Malmaison Bonaparte had seen Ris, and had favorably considered its purchase, and finally his choice had fallen upon a place in Bourgogne; moreover, he had not given her power of attorney. His brother Joseph was his business manager; it was through him that Josephine received her annual allowance of forty thousand francs, and to Joseph alone had Napoleon communicated his projects. The latter had advanced fifteen thousand francs on account to Lecoulteux; the receipt, however, which bore the date of 17th Messidor, year VII., was in the general's name, and Josephine therefore still owed fifteen thousand francs, because she had stipulated at marriage for the separation of property.

Nothing belonged to her; not even the hotel in the rue de la Victoire, for it had been bought and paid for by Bonaparte; all that she owned were the spoils of her Italian campaign, which she was pleased to display, and which one of her contemporaries tells us was worthy to have figured in " A Thousand and One Nights." She still possessed pictures, statues and antiques, but what were they against what she owed; and what did they amount to in comparison to what she was losing?

Thus Josephine was again in desperate straits and no longer at an age when she could hope to repair her fortunes by a lucky marriage. The years had left their traces, her figure remained supple and graceful, but her face had faded; a creole, married at sixteen, matured at twelve (for Tercier claims to have courted her in 1776) she was much older than a northern woman at the same period of life, and, looking the situation in the face, she clung to the hope that her husband would see her and be touched.

She went to the rue Chantereine, forced her way

into the house and to the door of the room in which Bonaparte had intrenched himself; but she knocked and implored vainly; finally she threw herself upon her knees, and the sounds of her sobs and lamentations rang through the house. She remained there for hours endeavoring to make him open the door; at last, utterly discouraged and exhausted, she was about to depart when her maid, Agathe Rible, thought of an expedient and begging her mistress to stop where she was, rushed for Eugène and Hortense, and returning with them had them kneel beside their mother and join their supplications with hers; at last the door opened, Bonaparte appeared, and without uttering a word held out his arms to his wife; his eyes were suffused with tears, and his face bore evidence of the terrible strain he had undergone.

It was no half pardon which was extended to Josephine, but forgiveness, utter and complete. Bonaparte had the wonderful faculty of forgetfulness, and once he had forgiven a fault and renewed his confidence, was able to erase from the tablets of his mind the faults or crimes which it had pleased him to condone, so that it was as though they had never been committed; not only did he forgive his wife, but, more wonderful, he ignored her accomplices; he never deprived one of them of life or liberty, did nothing to impede their success; nevertheless, when, by chance, he encountered certain of them he became suddenly extremely pale. He argued that those men were not to blame, but that the fault was his, for he had not taken good care of his wife, that she had not been properly guarded, but left too long alone and unprotected, and so another had been able to penetrate into his harem. It was natural, the necessity of sex ordered that man should be insistent, that woman should succumb; it was the law of nature. Bonaparte reasoned that if the erring wife was no longer beloved, she should be repudiated; if she was still dear, the only thing to do was to take her back; reproaches were senseless. Before an accomplished fact Bonaparte yielded, he accepted things as they were and people as he found them, and he did not exact of women a virginity which they did not possess. This is less French than Oriental in his nature, but so it was. Knowing, or fancying that he did, what to believe regarding the morality and virtue of women, convinced that marital security could be ensured only by watchfulness, he determined to take his precautions and to make it a rule that no man, under whatever pretext, was to remain alone with his wife, and to keep her constantly under surveillance. If this rule was not strictly adhered to with Josephine it was because he no longer hoped for offspring, and we shall see later how he managed with his second wife.

Josephine, triumphed over the Bonapartes, who having deplored the marriage, had desired, schemed for, and almost achieved a rupture. She made Napoleon contribute to her triumph, for on the following morning, when Lucien, the most ardent advocate of the divorce, called at an early hour in obedience to his brother's summons, he was ushered into Josephine's bed-chamber, where Napoleon was still in bed. The family realized that, having pardoned so much, Bonaparte would not wrangle over a question of money, and that it was useless to talk of his wife's debts, so for a time they subsided.

On the 21st of November he paid the one million, one hundred and ninety-five thousand francs due on the national bonds of the department of Dyle, later they served as a dowry for Marie-Adélaïde, commonly called Adèle, the natural daughter of M. de Beauharnais, for whom Josephine arranged a marriage with François-Michel-Auguste Lecomte, captain of infantry, and appointed collector at Sarlat immediately after the marriage. Napoleon also paid what was still owing on Malmaison, a bagatelle of two hundred and twenty-five thousand francs, and settled the tradespeople's accounts, amounting to one million, two hundred thousand francs; these he took the trouble to investigate, and it repaid him, for by deducting charges for goods which had never been delivered and righting overcharges he reduced the sum exactly one-half.

Josephine had cause for reflection; a husband who would thus pay debts to the amount of two million francs was a protector such as is not often found, and certainly one for whom a woman could well afford to make some sacrifices; she did so, and her apparent conduct up to the moment of her divorce gave her enemies no cause for gossip; she herself said that she was too afraid of losing her position to be indiscreet. She proved her gratitude to the Gohiers, for on the evening of the 17th of November she sent them an invitation to breakfast with the First Consul and herself on the following day, and, Gohier declining, she urged his wife to press upon him the acceptance of an important position under the new government. Gohier, always austere, indignantly refused; but when, after pouting for two years, he solicited the First Consul's favor, it was Josephine who obtained for him the position of commissary-general at Amsterdam, where he was so well contented that he remained for ten years, and would doubtless have passed the rest of his life if, in 1810, the post had not been abolished; it is said that then he refused to go to New York, but he later accepted a pension which was paid him during the restoration; nevertheless, he was a good republican to the end of his days and stipulated for a civil interment.

CHAPTER VII.

LA GRASSINI.

BONAPARTE had been able to forgive and forget, but he could not, in 1799, rekindle the passion he had felt for Josephine in his early manhood when, inexperienced in love or life, he had been intoxicated by the possession of a woman of rank. With Mme. Fourès he had tasted the charm and freshness of budding womanhood, and the comparison forced itself upon his memory; he had enjoyed the change, and had no longer either the desire, or the will to remain a faithful husband.

The relations which he wished Josephine to bear him in the future were rather those of a friend and confidante than a wife; he wished for a wise friend to whom, when in an expansive mood, he could tell some of the thoughts which agitated him, from whom he could seek advice regarding a society which he had had no time to study, and for a tender nurse who, should illness befall him, would give him almost maternal care, who would listen to, condole with, and coddle him ; upon whose bosom he could lay his aching head and be comforted as if he were a child. He wished her to be mistress as well as friend, a mistress with whom he need be under no restraint, who without apparent *ennui* would accept all his moods, cheer his melancholy or share his pleasures ; one who would always be ready for a journey, who would wait for but never keep him waiting, who, while not sharing his feverish activity would sympathize with all his undertakings ; who would drive with him behind the four horses he delighted to handle, follow his hunting expeditions, accompany him to the theatre, have a smile always on her lips and a gentle answer at her tongue's end.

For Josephine he reserved a special place in his political plans ; France, which he planned to reorganize, lacked, according to him, two of its primary elements, the nobility and the clergy ; he believed that he could rally the latter, and counted upon his wife to draw the former. Not taking into account the mysterious hierarchy to which the old society of France had submitted, the invisible lines which had divided it into diverse coteries, and the impassable gulf which separated them, he viewed it as a whole. Josephine, he thought, had been of it, and could draw it back to him ; she would be one with the *émigrés*, with the people of the old court and the nobility, with all those who belonged to the old *régime*, a natural intermediary between himself and them. Josephine could dispense benefits, distribute favors, repair injustices; little by little she could draw from the camp of the enemy those whom he wished to see re-enter the country; later she would serve as a link between what remained of the old *régime* and the new one he was building up.

Certainly, it was a fine and cleverly conceived rôle, and Josephine was apparently well qualified to play it; she had the necessary ease, elegance and grace of manner, possessed the happy faculty of speaking the right word in the right place, was exceptionally graceful and tactful in proffering a gift, and had a charming fashion of receiving people; she was possessed also of wonderful tact in address, which enabled her to approach people of all ranks and appear at ease in all company; what she lacked were those relations with the nobility upon which Bonaparte counted; those she had formed since the revolution would not serve his purpose, but would indeed have been injurious to the new government had not the First Consul from the first signified his intention of sundering them.

In the beginning Josephine found herself isolated,

but, in proportion as Bonaparte rose, obstacles fell away, social distinctions melted before him, and ambitions woke. In foreign lands and in France alike people set their wits about to discover, if by any lucky chance, they were even distantly connected with either the Beauharnais or Tascher families; they inquired into remote alliances and distant kinships until then unacknowledged, had recourse to inferiors and old family servants for information, and ere long a current set in which swept all the old titled, office-seeking, soliciting sycophants either towards the yellow salon of the Tuileries or the stucco drawing-room at Malmaison.

It must not be supposed that this state of affairs was due to Josephine, that it manifested itself because she was born a Tascher and married a Beauharnais; it existed solely because she was Mme. Bonaparte; people flocked around her because she was close to the master, the satellite of the planet from which they hoped for light, and they would have swarmed to toady her just the same no matter what her name, origin or past had been. Nevertheless, Josephine, perhaps sincerely, believed herself an important factor in the movement, and strove to impress Bonaparte with the invaluable service she rendered him, and, strange to relate, she succeeded in convincing him; as he firmly believed that *he* had conquered the clergy, he could easily believe that his wife had won the nobility.

What woman would not be proud to be raised to such a position, who would not have been satisfied with missions so diverse and so great? Had not the Consul the right to think that Josephine, with the memory of her infidelities and of all that had been forgiven her before her eyes, realizing the disparity in their ages and remembering the weaknesses to which she herself had yielded, would let pass *amours* which could neither detract from her position nor from her husband's affection, and that from fear lest Bonaparte be involved in a scandal and realizing what was due their position, she would always be extremely complaisant?

Josephine, unfortunately, failed to see matters in this light; not because she had become enamored of her husband's physical charms, nor because gratitude and admiration of his character had roused in her a love so profound that it rendered her jealous, but because she thought of her own interests, of *her* position. She reasoned that if Bonaparte detached himself from her physically he would end by divorcing her, and she lived in a state of perpetual apprehension; she watched him, and debased herself to set hired spies upon his track; she bored him with scenes, tears and hysterics, made a confidant of every one who would listen to her, and, in default of realities, imagined events which she recounted as facts, related incidents she would assert she had seen, and to the truth of which she would swear if needful.

The Consul's first gallantries, however, were not very serious. A day or two after his triumphal entry into Milan, the 14th or 15th Prairial, a concert was improvised, where, for his benefit, Italy's greatest artists, Marchesi and Grassini, sang. The latter was twenty-seven years of age (for she was born at Varèse in 1773), and she was no longer in appearance what she had been two years previous when, enthusiastically infatuated by Bonaparte, she had essayed to attract his attention and win him from Josephine. She was still handsome, but it was a style of beauty commonly seen in the streets of Italy; her figure was already over-developed, her face with its large features and black eyebrows, framed in thick black hair, looked a trifle heavy; her dark flashing eyes and swarthy skin gave her the appearance of a woman of amorous temperament, which, it appears, was deceptive. She had no end of lovers, not from sordid motives, for she was not mercenary, but resulting from mutual contempt and weariness; there was not one of them whom she had not proclaimed an angel at the beginning of the intimacy, but her honeymoons waned ere they had passed the first quarter.

Although Grassini's physical beauty was already on the decline, her artistic career was at its height; she was not a great musician, nor deeply versed in the principles of her art, but she was art itself; her contralto voice, always the most sympathetic of voices, was pure and smooth throughout its entire register. Hearing her, one listened not only to a great singer but a muse; no one phrased as she did, no one interpreted so understandingly grand opera (in opera bouffe she was wretched), no one deployed such amplitude of voice, such depth of expression in tragic rôles, or could so sway an audience.

Music was the only one of all the arts—above all, vocal music—for which Bonaparte had a particular taste; the rest he protected from policy, because he considered it incumbent upon his position and wished his name handed down to posterity as a patron of the arts; music alone he thoroughly appreciated, enjoyed and loved for itself and the pleasurable sensations it evoked; music calmed his nerves, charmed away melancholy, warmed his heart and set him a-dreaming. It matters little that he sung false, did not know a note and could not carry an air, he was so moved by music that he was carried out of himself, and that proves a higher appreciation of it than is felt by many claiming to be musicians. He valued fine singing so highly that he decorated the soprano Crescentini with the order of the Iron Crown.

In Grassini, it was less the woman than the songstress that captivated him. For two years Bonaparte had dwelt in her thoughts and her resistance was naturally not protracted. The day after the concert she breakfasted at the Consul's apartment, Berthier making a third, and it was settled that she should precede Bonaparte to Paris, where she should fill an engagement at the "Théâtre de la République et des Arts," and this arrangement was recounted in the fourth bulletin of the army in Italy; doubtless with the view of disarming Josephine's umbrage at the prima-donna's arrival.

The article read as follows: "The First Consul and the commander-in-chief (Berthier) attended a concert on the 15th Prairial, which, though improvised, proved very agreeable: Italian music has ever new charms. The celebrated Billington, Grassini and Marchesi are expected in Milan, and we are informed that they are shortly going to Paris to give concerts there."

This notice was printed for Josephine's benefit. Bonaparte dissimulated his infidelity behind a change of dates, and masked behind the name of

Billington, the only person in whom he took any interest.

At Milan, during the days which preceded Marengo, he spent every hour which he could spare in listening to Grassini. He was possessed by her marvellous voice, and held it to be the finest trophy of the campaign, and he wished that she should celebrate his triumphant return to France and sing his victories. He desired Grassini to be in Paris by the 14th of July for the fête of "La Concorde" and that she and the tenor Bianchi should sing an Italian duet. With this object in view he despatched an order to the minister of the Interior, desiring the composition of a song celebrating "The deliverance of the Cisalpine and the glory of our arms, a fine poem in Italian," insisted the Consul, "set to good music.

Twenty-three days later, in the church of Les Invalides, the Temple of Mars, which was magnificently decorated, official France assembled in solemn state to celebrate the nation's victories, and when the First Consul had taken his seat upon the platform, Grassini and Bianchi sang their duets, for there were two Italian numbers sung in succession. "Who could better," inquired the *Moniteur*, " celebrate the victory of Marengo than those to whom it assured peace and prosperity?"

It was audacious of Bonaparte to have his mistress sing at an official fête, and had the world suspected their relations there would certainly have been a clamor raised, but it seems their connection was then unknown, even Josephine being unsuspicious, for she placed reliance in the article in the army bulletin; moreover, the caprice, the physical caprice at least, was not of long duration. Before leaving Milan, Grassini, intoxicated by a success long and vainly desired, imagined that she was going to play a great rôle, not only in the theatre but in politics; she fancied that she had a great influence over her lover, and, being naturally good-natured, she left Italy laden with petitions from her compatriots.

Bonaparte was not a man who permitted any one to talk business when he desired to talk love, and Grassini bored him; moreover, he exacted that she should not show herself anywhere, but should live like a recluse in a little house in the rue Chantereine; this did not suit the lady at all, for she had dreamed of quite a different existence, of a *liaison à l'italienne*, which would have advertised at once her name, her person and her talent, and as fidelity was not her forte she was bored to death; there was not even a theatre open to her, for her terrible jargon closed the door of the opera, and at that time there was no Italian Opera in Paris, so she took to herself a lover in the person of Rode, the violinist. Bonaparte learned of her infidelity and severed his relations with her, but whatever fear Rode may have felt for his subsequent artistic career, neither he nor Grassini were made to suffer; twice even the Consul accorded them the Théâtre de la République for their concerts, the second of which was particularly brilliant, the box-receipts amounting to thirteen thousand eight hundred and sixty-eight francs and seventy-five centimes, and the account given of it by Suard in the *Moniteur* being almost lyric.

Later Giuseppina Grassini returned to the wandering life of a star, and came and went between Berlin, London, Milan, Genoa and Paris; she was fêted and flattered everywhere, and made engagements for three thousand pounds sterling for five months; nevertheless, when she passed through Paris and knocked at the door of the private apartment of the Tuileries it was always opened to her. The interviews led to nothing, but they distressed Josephine greatly. "I have learned," she wrote to one of her confidantes, "that Grassini has been ten days in Paris, and it seems that it is *she* who causes my present sufferings. I assure you, my dear, that if I were in the least to blame I would frankly admit it; you would do well to send Julie (her friend's maid) to watch and see if Grassini calls, try also to find out where the woman lives."

The whole nature of Josephine is revealed in this letter. What could Grassini matter to her? Did she not understand that there was no serious tie between the Italian and Bonaparte; that it was only one of those meetings wherein memory plays a greater part than desire? No, she had to pry and spy and address her complaints and her lamentations to a woman whom the Consul disliked and whom he had almost turned out of the Tuileries: such was Josephine.

She seems, however, to have calmed down in 1807, for when they were organizing the "chamber music," Napoleon recalled Grassini to Paris and offered the prima-donna, uniquely to the Primadonna, a fixed salary of thirty-six thousand francs, fifteen thousand francs of annual gratuities, without counting gifts, and fifteen thousand francs pension on her retirement; besides which she was to have the use of the Opera or *Les Italiens* once each winter in which to give herself a benefit; and was to use her vacations, if she chose, in travelling from city to city, advertising herself with her sonorous title as "Prima-donna to his Majesty the Emperor."

This title, however, did not serve to defend Grassini from the bandits who swarmed on the roads, and on the nineteenth of October, 1807, near Rouvrai on the confines of Yonne and the Côte d'Or, her travelling carriage was attacked by four deserters from a Swiss regiment and the poor creature was outraged, stripped and maltreated; but two days afterwards justice befell the aggressors and the Emperor admitted to the Legion of Honor M. Durandeau, commander of the national guard at Viteaux, who had slain two of the bandits and arrested a third. It is said that Grassini implored the bandits, who had taken a miniature of Bonaparte set in diamonds, to keep the jewels, but to return the miniature. It is recounted that, in a drawing-room where great indignation was expressed over Crescentini being decorated with the Iron Crown, Grassini exclaimed: "Ah, but you forget her wound!" (referring to the former's chagrin at her own appointment as first prima-donna to his Majesty.) A man of the world of that time tells us that La Grassini was clever and witty, spoke slangy French with a strong Italian accent, and that her habitual outspokenness gave her a reputation for sincerity and honesty.

Such was the situation from 1807 to 1814. Grassini received from the Emperor alone seventy thousand francs a year, which was more than she received from the public, for the latter became less enthusiastic with time, as was plainly shown at *Les Italiens* in November of 1813 when, with great ado, *Horace et les Curiaces* of Cimarosa was produced; but she always achieved a success at the "Théâtre de la Cour," and received the same consideration from the Emperor.

Gratitude was not one of La Grassini's virtues, nor were memory and affection characteristics of hers, for, after Napoleon's banishment to Saint Helena, she attached herself to his conqueror the Duke of Wellington and deployed her charms of voice and person for his benefit.

The "Iron Duke" had a fancy for that which Napoleon had praised, and it is related that he asked David to paint his portrait, to which request the artist replied "that he only painted historical subjects."

CHAPTER VIII.

FOOTLIGHT BEAUTIES.

BONAPARTE'S infatuation for Grassini was transitory, and Josephine's jealousy of brief duration; and although other actresses visited the Consul's private apartments in the Tuileries, their visits need not have caused her any great anxiety, for they were persons of mediocre virtue to whom Bonaparte could not become seriously attached, and of whom he simply required that they be pretty and complaisant during the few hours he passed in their company; but it sufficed that such callers came to the Tuileries, and the wife prowled about the staircases and corridors, candle in hand, with the hope of surprising them and enacting some scene which would put her husband plainly in the wrong.

Had it not been for Josephine, these passing fancies of the great conqueror would never have come to light; it was she who discovered and told of them; but, commonplace as these brief romances were, there is sufficient reason for reviewing them as they reveal certain phases of his character which might be vainly searched for elsewhere.

Aside from Grassini, and perhaps Mme. Branchu, who was so homely that to accuse him of a weakness for her would seem absurd were it not possible that the dilettante in him might have rendered her attractive because of the wonderful talent she displayed in tragic opera; he never affected the queens of the lyric stage.

No dancers visited the Tuileries, although it was the moment when dancers were in vogue; when Clotide was supported by Prince Pignatelli, who allowed her one hundred thousand francs a *month*, and was outbid by Admiral Mazaredo, who offered her four hundred thousand; when Bigottini was showered with favors from all sides, and thereby accumulated a fortune for her numerous progeny, for whom in later years she arranged advantageous marriages. No *comédiennes*, neither Mlle. Mars, who was not at all pretty when she made her *début*, nor Mlle. Devienne, the incomparable soubrette whose bright face betrayed her cleverness and wit, but who was unable to utter a word in answer to the flattering speech the Emperor once made her when *en route* for a hunt, nor Mlle. Mézeray, who was greatly interested in Lucien Bonaparte, nor yet Mlle. Gros, who made Joseph happy, ever went in at the famous "little door" of the Tuileries.

In 1808, Bonaparte may have been interested in Mme. Leverd, for after a single performance at Saint-Cloud she was admitted to the *Société Française*, and it would scarcely have been at the instigation of M. Rémusat the manager, for later, despite the Emperor's wishes and orders, he positively persecuted her. Mme. Leverd was an exceptionally graceful and charming woman, so sprightly, coquettish and bewitching that her lack of real talent was generally condoned; but if Napoleon had a fancy for her—which is not certain—she was the sole *comédienne* who appealed to him, for by nature, temperament and choice he was drawn to tragedians.

That was the most glorious period in the history of tragedy and the *Théâtre Français*, the time, when, before a highly-cultivated audience who would not permit the slightest inaccuracy to pass unnoticed; before soldiers who were in accord with noble and generous sentiments, a marvellous company kept alive the traditions of epic literature. While Bonaparte favored the actors with his protection, and was not sparing with money, he was severely critical; he held that the lines which they spoke were precepts for the nation and were of less importance for its literary education than for the formation of its morals. He once said to Goethe: "Tragedy should be the school of kings and people, it is the highest point a poet can attain." One evening on retiring he said: "Tragedy warms the heart and elevates the mind; it does, and should, create heroes," and it was then that he added: "If Corneille was alive I would make him a king."

Bonaparte did not care for melodrama, which he claimed had no proper place in dramatic literature, and had little taste for comedy, considering, like Molière and Beaumarchais, that it was unreal, agreeing with Le Sage that it was repulsive, and with Fabre d'Eglantine that it was pitifully unnatural; farce was utterly incomprehensible, and failed to distract him. Jokes, witticisms and cleverly turned phrases, even when they touched upon the main subject, but which were not, as he said, "the spirit of the thing," pretty phrases and graceful couplets all escaped him; he despised and disdained, or, rather, he ignored them. Tragedy seemed to him strong, serious, noble; his equals spoke in the kings, heroes and gods of tragedy, in their words he imagined he heard his own voice, for it was in such fashion that he wished to be represented to posterity, when, with the lapse of time, *his* life should be depicted on the stage.

Having this passion for tragedy Napoleon was naturally drawn in his hours of leisure to seek those who interpreted it; the pretty faces of the soubrettes, the affected innocence of the ingnéues, and the airs of the great coquettes could all be met at his court, the whole company of the social comedy were at his beck and call; but the women who impersonated Phedra, Andromache, Iphigenia and Hermione, were no longer courtesans but beings idealized by the characters they assumed, and viewing them at the play it was not the actress he desired, but the heroine she represented, and the artist's actual presence did not detract from this impression, the satisfaction of a purely sensual desire being hid from his eyes behind the shadow of poetry.

Recalled to reality by the press of business, having but a moment to give to the creatures of his fancy, unfamiliar with courteous phrases and unable to dissimulate the scorn he felt for those who, at a message from a valet, would rush to pamper his senses, Napoleon manifested, in both speech and action, a brutality which in another would have been pure cynicism: actually no one was less a cynic than he. "To everything pertaining to sensuality," says one of his intimate servitors, "he gave a poetic color and name;" even his brusqueness of speech dissimulated a certain embarrassment which he always felt in the presence of women. He professed a viciousness which he did not possess; thus, in conversation at Saint Helena, he wished to appear more familiar with sensations than sentiments, while in reality no one was more sentimental than he.

Desire in him did not have its rise in sensuality, but from an over-excited imagination, and it happened not infrequently, that by the time the fair one was at hand the current of his thoughts had changed, that he was occupied with affairs of state and anything which distracted him was a bore. A tap at the door was the signal that the expected guest had arrived: "Bid her wait," the Consul would exclaim. Upon a second, and impatient tap: "Bid her disrobe," the harassed Consul would command. At the third tap he lost all patience and would cry: "Send her away!" and then would return to his work.

Such was the experience, so we are informed, of Mlle. Duchesnois, but she was accustomed to such adventures. At the beginning of the consulate a young elegant, who had just inherited a fortune, invited some of his friends to celebrate his good luck at a country house in the environs of Saint Denis; they breakfasted, sang and played cards, then they began to feel bored, and the host sent to a well-known house in the Chaussée d'Antin for some of the gentler sex to enliven his guests. One of the young women remained without a gallant, being too plain to be attractive, although possessed of fine eyes, a svelt figure, an air of amiability and an expression of sadness which rendered her interesting; the party played at hide-and-seek in the park, and this girl, who was Mlle. Duchesnois, ran like a fawn, all her movements being graceful and supple, while her musical voice and clever conversation made her appear more intellectual and cultivated than her companions. Among the company was a young man who took pity upon her, conversed with her, and, finding her clever, cultivated her society and finally spoke of her to Legouvé who was curious to meet her, and who, on hearing her read some verses, was astonished at her talent.

Legouvé gave Mlle. Duchesnois advice and introduced her at Mme. de Montesson's where she met General Valence; he in turn became interested in her and promised to interest Mme. Bonaparte in her behalf and arranged for her début. She made her first appearance in Phedra, and it was not until a year or two later that her adventure at the Tuileries took place. Women have certain memories which nothing can obliterate, and Mlle. Duchesnois guarded throughout her life the apprehension that the words so often heard in her early youth and in the days of servitude, "she is *too* ugly," would again ring in her ears.

Thérèse Bourgoin was also dismissed in the same unceremonious manner, but she who so insolently answered: "Neither seen nor heard of," in response to a letter of inquiry from a duchess of the Empire and wife of a marshal of France regarding a lost parrot, was not likely to accept such treatment in a spirit of humility, particularly when the affront to her vanity was augmented by a personal loss— that of a rich lover, the minister of the Interior, Chaptal. After Thérèse Bourgoin's second appearance, in which she had been greatly harassed, Chaptal secured an engagement for her at the Théâtre Français, and to confirm this favor he wrote a public and official letter to Mlle. Dumesnil, announcing the bestowal of a ministerial gratuity and thanking her for having profitably used the leisure of her retirement in the formation of such a pupil. Mlle. Dumesnil, at his request, gave the débutante some worldly advice, and Chaptal and the young actress were to be seen everywhere together; he placed the newspapers at her orders, and gave Paris food for scandal. Mlle. Bourgoin was just suited to a man of fifty; she had an ingenuous air and roguish smile, clear, infantile eyes, which gave her an appearance of innocence, a ringing voice and spiciness of speech, which, combined, gained for her the appellation of "the goddess of joy and pleasure."

Chaptal's great mistake lay in disregarding appearances and so compromising himself; blinded by Mlle. Bourgoin's specious manner, he believed implicitly in her fidelity; a belief of which Napoleon was malicious enough to disabuse him. One evening, when he had a business engagement with the minister, he also made an appointment with Mlle. Bourgoin, and the actress was announced within Chaptal's hearing; Napoleon sent word that she must wait, and a little later excused himself entirely, but Chaptal, on hearing his mistress announced, had gathered up his papers and departed, and he sent in his resignation that same night. The young woman on her side openly declared war, and at St. Petersburg, where she went after the peace of Tilsit, she regaled her adorers with all the epigrams and lampoons regarding the Emperor which were amusing Paris.

At Erfurt the Emperor took *his* revenge and entertained the Czar with epigrams on Mlle. Bourgoin, warning him against her over-generosity in affairs of the heart, which naturally militated against her success. At the restoration she espoused the royalist cause, all the more intensely because she had been presented to the king by the Duke de Berry and had good reasons for clinging to the Bourbons. During the hundred days she did not hesitate to array herself in their colors, for which no one interfered with her, but as the Duke de Berry failed to renew their relations on his return, her enthusiasm died a natural death.

Although Napoleon's relations with Mesdames Duchesnois and Bourgoin were unimportant, it was not the same with Mlle. George. Napoleon was installed at Saint-Cloud when Mlle. George visited him for the first time; she was received in the small apartment opening into the orangery, and it is claimed that it was on this occasion that he stung her pride by saying: "You must have hideous feet for you keep your stockings on." Her animal beauty was so perfect in every other respect that this defect struck Napoleon's eye and so impressed him that the remark escaped involuntarily.

No one was more keenly alive to the beauty of well-modelled feet and hands than Bonaparte; it was one of the first things that he looked at in a woman, and when they were ill-formed he used to say: "Her extremities are common." Such was the case with Mlle. George, who, at seventeen, was superbly handsome, whose head, shoulders, arms and body were fit for a painter's model, but whose extremities, particularly the feet, were very ugly; doubtless the coarse, ill-made shoes which she had worn when sweeping her father's doorsteps at Amiens had helped to deform them. The father was manager of a theatre and led its orchestra.

Napoleon passed nearly the whole of that winter at Saint-Cloud, and Mlle. George was frequently his guest; aside from admiring her beauty, he was entertained by her cleverness and aptness at repartee; she recounted to him all the stories, and imitated for him the actions of the habitués of the Théâtre Français, and in those days there were lots of good stories going about. Her visits were continued after he returned to Paris, where he received her in an apartment of the *entresol* at the Tuileries; he never went to her house, and so never encountered Coster de Saint-Victor, or any other of her lovers. Mlle. George claimed that her intimacy with Napoleon endured for two years, and that during all that time she was absolutely faithful: it was more than was expected of her.

Josephine soon learned of this affair, was unusually disquieted by it, and treated her husband to innumerable scenes. "She worries a great deal more than is called for," wrote Bonaparte; "she is always fearful that I may fall seriously in love; can she not understand that love is not for me? Love is a passion which makes one willing to abandon everything for the sake of the beloved person; certainly I am not of a nature to give myself up so completely, and what can it then matter to Josephine that I amuse myself with women for whom I feel no such sentiment?"

No one could reason better, but reason went for nothing with Josephine. She was obliged to acknowledge, however, that Napoleon was very discreet; there was no scandal, no favors shown Mlle. George as an actress, for when she failed to keep her engagement she was rudely enough menaced with imprisonment and knew that the threat was not an idle one; when she played at court she received the same fee as her comrades, and it is said that when she made bold enough to ask Napoleon for his portrait he handed her a double Napoleon, saying: "Here it is, and said to be a good likeness."

Probably he gave her money, for on the books of the privy purse the item, "handed to His Majesty the Emperor," is frequently repeated, designating sums of from ten to twenty thousand francs, although nothing indicates the uses for which they were destined; on one occasion only, the 16th of

August, 1807, does Mlle. George's name appear on these books, against a gift of ten thousand francs, but three years had then elapsed since the cessation of her visits to the Tuileries, and this present was doubtless simply a memento presented on her saint's day. Less than a year later, on the 11th of May, 1808, Mlle. George left Paris surreptitiously in company with Duport, an opera dancer, who, fearing to be arrested at the barriers, had disguised himself as a woman. Ignoring alike her engagement at the Théâtre Français and her creditors, she fled to Russia to rejoin a lover, who, they say, had promised to marry her; this lover was Benckendorff, brother of the Countess d'Liéven, who came to Paris in the suite of the ambassador Tolstoi; he had just been recalled and purposed to show off his mistress in St. Petersburg, and above all before the Czar.

Underlying all this there was quite an intrigue, the object of which was to win the Czar from Mme. Narishkine, by a brief *liaison* with the French actress, from which, it was thought, he could be easily lead back to the Empress. Mlle. George most assuredly suspected nothing of these fine schemes, and in letters to her mother she expatiated upon the charms of her " good Benckendorff," and signed herself, in August of 1808, " George Benckendorff." She was presented to the Emperor Alexander who gave her a handsome diamond ornament and had her called to Peterhoff, but she was never asked the second time; she claimed that the grand duke, who, after a performance of Phedra, said: "Your Mlle. George is not worth as much in her way as my charger in his," visited her daily and "loved her as a sister."

According to her, the Russian nobility and gentry alike were her adorers, but this was not the end the conspirators had in view when they encouraged her going to St. Petersburg, nor was it what Napoleon had permitted them to plan when the plot had been revealed to him; nevertheless, when, in 1812, Mlle. George desired to return to France and rushed to rejoin the principal actors of the *Société Française* who had been summoned to Dresden during the armistice, the Emperor not only had her reinstated in the society, but ordered that she should receive a salary for the six years of absence; her comrades never forgave that.

During the hundred days Mlle. George sent word to Napoleon that she could give him papers which would compromise the Duke d'Otrante, and Napoleon sent a trusted messenger to her; on his return he asked: "Did not mademoiselle tell you that her affairs were very much embarrassed?" "No, sire," replied the messenger, "she only spoke of her desire to hand those papers personally to your Majesty." "I already know what they refer to, Caulaincourt has mentioned them," returned the Emperor, "and he told me also that Mlle. George was in straitened circumstances ; you are to give her twenty thousand francs from my private purse."

Mlle. George at least was grateful, and undoubtedly the sentiments which she frankly avowed militated against her, and caused her brutal expulsion from the Théâtre Français. Even in her old age, when nothing remained either in face or figure of the one time triumphant beauty, her voice trembled when she spoke of Napoleon, and she manifested such unfeigned emotion that she deeply impressed the young men who listened to her, and it was not the lover whom she lauded, but the Emperor. This woman, not from the prudery of old age, for she spoke freely enough of other lovers, but from a sort of awe, seemed to forget that Napoleon had ever found her beautiful and sought her love, and she spoke not of the man he had been for her, but of the man he had been for France. Mlle. George reminds one of one of those nymphs whom the gods honored by a brief caress, and who, blinded by the heavenly effulgence, failed to see the face of the deity.

CHAPTER IX.

READERS.

TRAGEDIANS alone climbed the dark staircase, and under the guidance of Constant or Roustam traversed a gloomy corridor, lighted night and day by argand lamps, and finally reached a room in the *entresol* from which a secret staircase led to Bonaparte's private apartments. Every morning Mme. Bernard, the imperial florist, placed a bouquet in this room, there was an appropriation of six hundred francs a year for that express purpose, but the flowers, which were renewed daily, died less quickly than the sentiment which inspired the visitors.

As Bonaparte rose in power these visitors—the solicitous, the ambitious, the intriguants—became so numerous that it would be impossible to keep count of them all. Every man who fills a position of power finds himself solicited by like callers, who await only a sign to give themselves to him, and, keeping themselves constantly in view, beg for a glance, seeking a profitable dishonor. Napoleon

NAPOLEON.

was thirty in 1800, thus, up to 1810, he was in the prime of life, and in vigorous health; he neither sought nor shunned amours, but, aside from Josephine, only two women ever inspired him with deep affection; he thought but moderately well of the sex, none of them ever interfered with his work, distracted his thoughts, retarded his progress or caused a modification of his plans; and these little episodes were not unlike the supper which was nightly set out for him upon one end of his writing-table: he would not have taken a step to procure food, but, finding it at hand, very naturally partook of it, and at once returned to his work. The important fact is not that a few veiled women stole by night into the Emperor's secret apartment, but that no woman, wife or mistress, habitually frequented the study and the ministerial cabinet.

If Napoleon were not the person in question, if certain of his *liaisons* had not been recounted with details invented at pleasure, and if some of his favorites had not become authors, either for the pecuniary profit accruable from their memoirs, or for the pleasure of appearing before the public in a rôle they had never played, it would hardly be worth while to take note of these transitory love-affairs, but the calumnies have been too widely spread to render the *truth* unimportant.

One of the women who have become best known as a writer, and who received innumerable favors from both Consul and Emperor, must still escape censure; for circumstantial evidence, no matter how convincing, should not replace positive proof, and the study of characters analogous to hers will place her in the rank she should occupy.

Another, much less celebrated, but who up to the present time has done good service to pamphleteers, is a certain Mme. de Vaudey, who, when the Empire was proclaimed, was named lady-in-waiting on the strong recommendation of M. Lecoulteux de Canteleu. She was well-born, being the daughter of that remarkable soldier, Michaud d'Arçon, who invented the floating batteries used at the siege of Gibraltar, furnished the plans for the campaign in Holland in 1793, took Bréda without striking a blow, and was one of the most prominent senators of the council; she was well connected, also, for her husband, M. de Barberot de Vellexon, Lord of Vaudey and captain in the royal Bourgundians, was descended from an old Alsatian family, residents of Gray since the fifteenth century; moreover, she was an extremely pretty person, sparkling with wit and unusually clever, sang exquisitely, and wrote even better. Mme. de Vaudey was appointed lady-in-waiting in 1814, and as the Empress was about starting to take the waters at Aix-la-Chapelle, she accompanied her; and when Napoleon, early in September, rejoined Josephine at Aix, for the triumphal journey on the Rhine, Mme. de Vaudey accompanied them everywhere, and employed her time in amusing His Majesty. On her return to Paris she thought herself in a position to brave the Empress, whose jealousy was aroused, and to set up housekeeping on the footing of a favorite in a pretty little château near Auteuil where she entertained largely, gave fêtes, lived like a princess, and, following her imperial mistress' example, ran deeply into debt. Once, after a prolonged audience, she laid the state of her finances before the Emperor, and her debts were paid; a second disclosure of her pecuniary embarrassment met with the same success; but when she petitioned for a third audience, Napoleon refused downright to see her. "I have not," he said to Duroc, "either sufficient money nor good-nature to pay such a price for what I can get so cheaply; thank Madame de Vaudey for the kindness she has shown me, and never mention her to me again."

On the receipt of this message Mme. de Vaudey wrote a pathetic letter, declaring that she would poison herself if her debts—debts of honor!—were not paid in twenty-four hours. The aide-de-camp on duty was hastily dispatched to Auteuil, and found the lady disposed for anything—except suicide ;—it was immediately requested that she send in her resignation as lady-in-waiting, and that is why her name does not appear on the imperial almanac.

Some years later, after her mind had become unbalanced, Mme. de Vaudey called upon M. de Polignac and offered to assassinate Napoleon ; later still, reduced to destitution, almost blind and with a paralyzed arm she peddled her *Souvenirs du Directoire et de l'Empire* as a pretext for asking assistance, and it was she who furnished Ladvocat, the librarian, with the greater part of his *Memoires d'une dame du Palais* ; but she was in want and mentally unbalanced, others had not the same excuse. It was Josephine who, on the solicitation of Lecoulteux, had introduced Mme. de Vaudey at court, and she had numberless protégés of the same, and of an inferior order, none of whom merited her patronage and who appear to have had no other reason for being at court than their willingness to cater to Napoleon's fancies.

This state of affairs was not premeditated by Josephine, but her creole nature had need of companionship and distraction ; she liked to surround herself with agreeable and compliant people who were neither her equals nor yet servants, whose pretty faces pleased her eye, whose conversation amused, and whose accomplishments helped to distract her, who, in short, peopled pleasantly the palace wherein she claimed she lived in sad and solitary state; she engaged them without making many inquiries, sometimes touched by a sad story, sometimes attracted by a pretty face or an unexpectedly bright response. These young women, from some of whom the bloom of innocence had already been rubbed by friction with the world, were all hoping for conquests; poor and not educated to entertain conscientious scruples, they were thrown suddenly into the midst of a court which was one of the most splendid in history, and in the long idle days which they spent in the Empress' private apartments they had nothing to do but accept the attentions of the officers with whom they constantly came in contact and to angle for husbands. Naturally they aspired to find husbands among the officers who thronged the palace, as so many women no better than themselves had done; women who were then wives of marshals of the Empire; they saw constantly and familiarly him from whom emanated all favors, who at a sign could make or destroy one's fortune, and put themselves in his way, ambitious for that sign, ready to risk anything in order to obtain it; they were complaisant, presented themselves only when desired, and exerted themselves to please, and as the subalterns kept a sharp lookout to see if the Emperor admired any of them, arrangements were speedily concluded and affairs followed their natural course without the slightest attempt at seduction on one side, or the least love on the other. But, no matter how carefully concealed the intrigue, Josephine always discovered it; then there was a scene, and the young person was discharged; however, she had usually received a good dot and was apt to crown her career by marriage with some gentleman who was not over-scrupulous, and thus become the progenitor of people of some importance.

A typical case was that of Félicité Longory, daughter of a petty officer of the cabinet, whom Josephine had called to fill the position of lady usher. As such she was stationed in the salon into which the private apartments opened, and her duties consisted simply of throwing open the double doors for the passage of the Emperor or Empress; for this service she received three thousand, six hundred francs a year, which sum Josephine supplemented by six hundred francs in 1806. Félicité was a personage of no importance, almost a servant, yet she succeeded in attracting the attention of the Emperor, and, the inevitable scene with the Empress ensuing, was naturally discharged, and later married well.

Mlle. Lacoste stood a little higher on the social plane. She was a slight and pretty blonde, an orphan without fortune, who had been brought up by an aunt who was said to be a schemer, and who managed her niece's presentation to Josephine. The Empress, touched by the girl's forlorn state, gave her an ambiguous position, vaguely entitled a reader. Mlle. Lacoste certainly did not find her duties fatiguing, for hardly had she assumed the position when the court departed for Milan where the coronation was to take place, and she followed the court, without being of it, for she had no clearly defined position. As reader, Mlle. Lacoste was denied access to the drawing-room of the ladies-in-waiting; and, too well-bred to associate with the ladies' maids, near to whom, however, she was lodged, she felt isolated and forlorn in her new surroundings. At Stupinitz the Emperor caught sight of her and remarked her pretty face; at Milan he spoke to her and an understanding was arrived at. Josephine, however, soon became aware of it and there was a terrible scene; the reader was ordered to leave and her aunt summoned from Paris to escort her home; but before her departure the Emperor insisted that she should appear once at least among the Empress' retinue. This created a great scandal, for a reader was not supposed to appear outside the private apartments. On returning to Paris Napoleon undertook to find a husband for Mlle. Lacoste, and married her to a rich financier; she made an honest wife and devoted mother, and never reappeared at the Tuileries.

During this same journey to Italy, in the midst of the fêtes given at Genoa in celebration of the union of France and the Ligurian Republic, a lady by name of Gazzani or Gazzana (her name has been written both ways), crossed Napoleon's path; she was the daughter of a Mme. Bertani, a dancer, or, according to some historians, a singer connected with the Grand-Théâtre.

Out of compliment to Josephine a number of Italian ladies had gone to Milan, and it had been arranged that La Gazzani should accompany them; it was a strangely assorted party, comprising ladies of the Negrone, Brignole, Doria and Remedi families, and women like Mme. Gazzani and Bianchina La Flèche, who was destined to such a brilliant career in Westphalia.

Carlotta Gazzani was tall, rather too slight perhaps, but with a most graceful and elegant carriage; her hands and feet were not remarkable for their beauty, indeed she invariably wore gloves, but her features were of the purest type of Italian beauty and her eyes large, dark and very brilliant. Even women praised La Gazzani's beauty, which is positive proof that it was great, but also, that she lacked that peculiar and indescribable charm which renders some women so captivating and the envy of all their sex. Mme. Rémusat admitted that it was her husband, then first chamberlain, who charged himself with the Italian beauty's introduction at court, and who persuaded the Emperor to nominate her reader to Josephine ; evidently it was not Talleyrand alone who, as Napoleon once said, "always had his pocket full of mistresses."

Mme. Gazzani, then called Mme. Gazzani Brentano, and who long afterwards assumed the title of Baroness de Brentano, replaced Mlle. Lacoste, at a salary of five hundred francs a month ; from 1805 to 1807 little was heard of her, for during that period which comprised the battle of Austerlitz and the campaign in Prussia and Poland the Emperor was little in France, but on his return to Paris and later at Fontainebleau she saw her opportunity and seized it. She was so lodged that she could easily reach the Emperor at all hours, and when summoned by him immediately hastened to obey. She never attempted to pose as a favorite, but accepted with modesty her rôle of occasional mistress, and the Empress, at first inclined to be jealous, was quickly reassured by Napoleon's making her his confidante. The Italian retained a respectful and submissive attitude towards the Empress, and remained unpretentiously in her place. She was accorded the entrée of the drawing-room reserved for the ladies-in-waiting, but, that favor bestowed, Napoleon did not publicly interest himself in her and permitted the ladies of the palace to treat her as they pleased and shun her if they chose ; their hostility, however, was of a short duration, and soon several of them, and not the least haughty, relented sufficiently to admit her into their circle. Mme. Gazzani obtained something more substantial, however, from her relations with the Emperor than the flatteries of the court, as she secured the general receivership at Évreau for her husband.

After the imperial divorce Mme. Gazzani rejoined her lord, and being close to Navarre, where Josephine was residing, she became an intimate of the household to which she was strongly attracted by a *liaison* with M. de Pourtalès, a groom of the Empress' household. Her intimacy with the Emperor terminated at Fontainebleau, after that he only saw her by chance. He never loved her and appears never to have talked of her, but she was consoled for his forgetfulness by the success in life of her daughter, Charlotte-Josephine-Eugénie-Claire, self-styled Baroness de Brentano, who made a brilliant match and married M. Alfred Mosselman, by whom she had a daughter who married M. Eugène Le Hon.

Although oblivious of Mme. Gazzani, Napoleon often spoke of a certain Mlle. Guillebeau, the daughter of a bankrupt banker, who was, in 1808, appointed to assist Mme. Gazzani as reader. Mlle. Guillebeau's mother was Irish by birth, and had three daughters, two of whom were grown and contributed to the family income by dancing and playing the tambourine in the drawing-rooms of the nobility. The eldest compassed an introduction to the Princess Elisa, who assisted her to make a good marriage, and the younger, who the gossips affirmed had not been cruel either to Murat or Junot, was clever enough to secure the protection of Queen Hortense, who was taken with her pretty face and clever dancing. At a masquerade ball, given by Caroline at the Elysée, Hortense, who was to lead a costumed quadrille, took a fancy to dress Mlle. Guillebeau as Folly, and to have her, tambourine in hand, lead the procession of her maidens into the ball-room. Caroline had double reasons for jealousy, and as soon as she perceived Mlle. Guillebeau she rushed to Hortense's side and a lively scene ensued, which resulted in Folly's dismissal from the ball-room. This was an episode in the continual warfare which raged between the Bonapartes and the Beauharnais, and to avenge both herself and her favorite, Hortense presented Mlle. Guillebeau to her mother, who, to annoy Caroline, attached the girl to herself in the position of reader.

This incident occurred just previous to the journey to Bayonne, and when the imperial household was installed at Marrac, Mlle. Guillebeau found herself in an isolated position; court etiquette closed the door of the drawing-room against her during the day, and she only entered it occasionally of an evening in order to entertain the company with her music and dancing, and was therefore reduced to passing most of the time in her bedroom, which was in reality nothing better than a garret, for the château of Marrac was small, and had not been constructed with a view to lodging an imperial household. Being a great coquette, the girl was fearfully bored, and was well content when a servant—a Mamaluke—tapped at her door and announced an imperial visit. Matters were progressing quite to her taste when Lavallette, who, by right of his position of postmaster-general, watched the correspondence of the household, sent Napoleon a letter written to Mlle. Guillebeau by her mother, in which she had clearly traced the rôle her daughter had to play, and recommended her to lose no occasion to make herself agreeable to His Majesty, and to strengthen his fancy for her to the utmost; pointing out to the girl how greatly to her interest it was to follow this course, and how she could profit by the imperial weakness. Napoleon was so disgusted with the lowness of the intrigue, in which he afterwards discovered that Prince de Bénévant was implicated, that he immediately commanded a postchaise for mademoiselle, and she was packed off to Paris escorted only by a valet.

Mlle. Guillebeau met and married a M. Sourdeau who, thanks to the Emperor, was given a receivership, but he appropriated the funds and prison stared him in the face when the restoration occurred and proved his salvation. Mme. Sourdeau was clever enough to secure an introduction to the Duke de Berry, who found her "charming and possessed of the most beautiful eyes in the world," and as a recompense for favors received appointed her husband consul at Tangier.

In the life of Napoleon, these passing fancies count for little; they barely appealed to his senses, never touched his heart; they give us no insight to the active side of his nature, but demonstrate his hatred of intrigue, his generosity and certain of his habits. It would be easy to relate many adventures of the same kind, but none more interesting; tales of garrison adventures for which, as Emperor, he paid two hundred napoleons where one of his captains would have paid twenty francs; he was not constituted differently than his marshals and his soldiers; he was a man, but he was not a man whose senses were so imperious that he was always forced to yield to them.

At Vienna he observed a young girl, who, on her side, was apparently infatuated with him; he had her followed, and invited her to visit him in the evening at Schoenbrunn; she accepted, and as she spoke only Italian and German they conversed in the former language. Napoleon discovered almost immediately that the girl belonged to a most respectable family and did not comprehend in the least what the invitation to meet him implied, and that while she felt a passionate admiration for him it was ingenuous and innocent; he ordered that she should be immediately reconducted to her home, and provided for her future, giving her a dot of twenty thousand florins.

This act was far from being unique in Napoleon's history, it was repeated three times at least in his life; on the last occasion at Saint Helena.

CHAPTER X.

JOSEPHINE'S CORONATION.

In the idleness and disquietude of her daily life, which resembled closely that of an aged sultana, Josephine had ample leisure for reflection, and the outgrowth of her continual agitation, anxiety and jealousy was the knowledge that by one thing only could her position be secured—the birth of a child. Without understanding Napoleon's ambitious projects, she yet knew that he had a consuming desire for male issue, and, as his fortunes rose, gradually comprehended why he so desired an heir, and realized that for her maternity should no longer be a pretext for obtaining favors in the shape of journeys which gave her relaxation from the monotonous life at the Tuileries—but an aim ; that the throne of which her husband was slowly climbing the steps *should* have an assured heir.

To Bonaparte, chief of a republic, Bonaparte reestablishing the Bourbons and content with a lifelong place of honor under the restored monarchy, a son was not indispensable, but, unfortunately for Josephine, the contingent glory of a rôle à la Monk did not tempt him, nor the disinterestedness of a life like Washington's satisfy him. A great flood of opinion, one of those popular currents which nothing stems, swept all obstacles from his path and raised him first to a consulate which was republican, later to one which was autocratic and differed from a monarchy only in name, and above all in the insolvable question of heredity.

Around this question of heredity surged the ambitions of some and the projects of others. Josephine saw that Bonaparte's brothers already aspired to the succession; that the sisters debated whether their husbands, too, might not have a chance, and that the nation itself desired, after so much turbulence, a government that would endure more than a lifetime; but if a monarchal form of government was established, who was to succeed Napoleon? There were the Consul's brothers, but by what right could they be called to the throne? An hereditary monarchy in its Christian form is a derivative of the Hebrew form of government, and is supposedly a divine institution, but it applies exclusively to the chief of a dynasty and his descendants, however far removed, provided that they are male and descended in direct line from him. In order that Napoleon's brothers should succeed him it would have been necessary to have recourse to an expedient, common enough with the ancients, and proclaim that the late Charles de Buonaparte had been emperor of France, but it was unlikely that the country would accept such a fiction.

Another expedient was to abandon the Hebraic law of succession and institute the Roman law of adoption; under that *régime* the Consul would be free to choose as his successor whomsoever he judged best fitted to fill his place; but it was a question whether the nation would overcome its prejudice in favor of the old monarchal system and accept such a solution of the problem. The simplest, most natural solution, which would both annihilate the ambitions and please the populace, was the birth of a son to Napoleon.

In her anxiety to give to her husband the heir so ardently desired Josephine visited innumerable mineral springs whose waters were supposed to cure sterility, consulted various physicians and submitted heroically to any treatment recommended, made pilgrimages, and even had recourse to sorcerers; whenever she had the least ground for believing herself with child she immediately made Bonaparte a sharer in her joyous hopes, and he in turn confided his happiness to his intimates; as each hope died

Napoleon became more and more morose, and indulged in hard and bitter speeches which attested his disappointment. Once at Malmaison, he decided to get up a hunt in the park, when Mme. Bonaparte came to him weeping and said: "How can you think of hunting in the park when all our animals are with young?" at which he retorted in a loud voice: "Well, then, I suppose it must be abandoned; everything here seems to be prolific except the mistress?"

Publicly he threw all the blame for their childlessness upon his wife; but recalling Mme. Fourès and many others, none of whom had borne him children, he entertained secret doubts of the justice of the aspersion he cast upon her; doubts which Josephine stimulated by talking incessantly of *her* children, and by forcing Eugène and Hortense constantly upon his notice; she harped so much upon the subject that Mme. Bacciochi lost all patience, and one day silenced her by remarking: "There may be something in what you say, but remember, sister, when those children saw the light you were much younger than you are now!"

The majority of the family, however, were prevailed upon to accept her view of the situation, and Napoleon himself did not combat it vigorously. On several occasions he said to his brother Joseph:

"I am childless, you all think me impotent, and Josephine, despite her anxiety, is not likely to bear children now; so after me the deluge!"

When, on his return from Spain, Lucien preached divorce, and suggested the advisability of a marriage with an Infanta, Napoleon rejected the proposition; undoubtedly he had diverse motives for so doing, but possibly the strongest of all was of a personal and private nature; he may have reasoned that while a union with a Bourbon princess would unquestionably further his ambitious schemes, it was foolish to struggle for a throne if unable to transmit his name and glory to a son.

The Spanish union was nevertheless urged by Lucien, for whom Josephine had but scant affection, remembering that he had been the first advocate of a divorce, and from that time she made no further effort to conciliate her husband's brothers, but did not hesitate to report any story which might injure them, however false, nor to embellish the truth; and she was not sorry when a rupture finally occurred. Napoleon often said of Josephine that "she bears no more malice than a pigeon," but this was true only when her personal interests were not at stake.

Although the doubt which she had inspired in Napoleon served to avert a divorce in 1801, Josephine knew herself to be at the mercy of chance; it was neither the actresses whose company he frequented, nor the ladies of the court whom she feared, for if one of them happened to bear a child she reasoned that Napoleon could not be assured of his fatherhood unless a striking physical resemblance proved it; what she dreaded was a *liaison* similar to the one with Mme. Fourès, for a child born under such conditions meant the shipwreck of all her hopes and ambitions, as Bonaparte had reached a point where he felt himself upon a level with the old dynasties, and knew that a union with him would not be disdained by the purest blood of France, while there was no lack of men like Talleyrand, "the accursed limper," ready to tempt him, suggest advantageous marriages and act as intermediary.

In default of a child, which alone, as Napoleon himself said, "could insure Josephine's peace of mind and put a stop to her unceasing jealousy," how could she attach herself to her husband so firmly that he would not dream of breaking the chain? For years associated with him in his public life, received everywhere as a sovereign, holding her salon at the Tuileries or at Saint-Cloud, obliged by Napoleon himself to take precedence over all other women, even above his mother at family and informal gatherings, presented to the country and to Europe as the first lady in France, she could not be repudiated without a scandal, and such a proceeding would certainly be badly received by the public. She had been the medium for the distribution of too many favors, had exercised her influence to obtain too many pardons, not to have warm and faithful adherents; but, as Napoleon's popularity grew and his power increased, the worldly prestige of his wife diminished, and she realized more and more that no tie could bind him to her save a living token of their union.

Josephine finally conceived a most ingenious plan, namely, to constitute a heredity by persuading Napoleon to adopt his nephew and her grandson, the child of Louis Bonaparte and Hortense de Beauharnais; such a procedure would conciliate all factions, satisfy the Bonapartes, because the heir-presumptive would be one of their name, and assure her own future, and the question of succession would then be settled. She convinced Napoleon of the wisdom of this law and he spoke of it to Louis; but Louis indignantly refused invoking the rights of his brother Joseph and himself, and before these imaginary and baseless claims, which were without precedent in history and totally at variance with the monarchal doctrine, Napoleon gave way and renounced the sole expedient which would have enabled him to establish an heredity without having recourse to divorce.

Failing to achieve the adoption of her grandson, Josephine saw no other means of consolidating the tie which linked her to Napoleon and his fortunes, and while suffering the greatest disquietude she was obliged to accept the situation with such fortitude as she could summon to her aid.

The First Consul being proclaimed Emperor, she naturally became Empress, received the homage of the ministers of state and was addressed as "Your Majesty," and after the triumphal journey from Aix-la-Chapelle to Mayence, after the cannons of the Invalides had announced her return to the Parisians and the authorities had defiled before her throne, her position seemed assured, and a divorce highly improbable; but her own jealousy nearly occasioned the dreaded calamity.

At Saint-Cloud she observed that a lady who had called to pay her respects, left the apartment sooner than was strictly in accordance with court etiquette, and having long suspected an undue intimacy between this lady and the Emperor, she herself left the drawing-room and mounted the secret stairway leading to the private apartment in the *entresol* where he was in the habit of receiving fair visitors, and, recognizing the lady's voice, she insisted upon being admitted and made a scene which provoked Napoleon to violent anger. As a result he declared himself weary of such espionage and determined to end it, and saying that he should follow the counsels of his friends and secure a divorce, he sent for Eugène to arrange the details. Eugène arrived, but both for his mother and himself he declined all favors or any pecuniary assistance; thus several days passed, Eugène remained unapproachable, while Josephine did not recriminate, but wept unceasingly, and Napoleon's resolution weakened before her tears; moreover, he knew himself to be in the wrong, and that it was not thus so grave an act should be accomplished, and a final conversation took place between them. "I have not the courage," said he at its close, "to carry my threat into execution, and if you will only be affectionate and obedient I shall never *oblige* you to leave me, but I will admit that I wish that you yourself would relieve me from the embarrassment of our present relations."

Josephine, however, had no taste for self-sacrifice, and did not propose to decide her fate, Napoleon must be the arbiter; she was ready to obey, but she intended to await his order to descend the steps of the throne to which he had raised her. Influenced by his habits, political uncertainty, the hope of a possible paternity, affection for his stepchildren, the necessity of ruining the life which he had linked with his, of renouncing forever the woman whom he still loved, touched by the resignation of the Beauharnais family, and provoked at the joy manifested by Josephine's enemies, Napoleon once more abandoned the idea of divorce, and, as though to prevent its return, commanded his wife to give serious attention to the preparations for his coronation, in which she should be associated.

Certainly Josephine should have been content; her most ambitious dreams could never have reached this height; she, the creole, who had been brought to France owing to the caprice of a courtesan, was to realize the ambitious dreams of past queens of France, be crowned by the Pope, and participate in the triumphs of the new Charlemagne.

She was, however, desirous of forging still another link in the chain which bound Napoleon to her. For eight years she had been perfectly content with the civil ceremony which alone cemented their union, but it now occurred to her that the benison of the Church would lend additional strength to her position. She did not ignore the fact that she would have great obstacles to surmount before overcoming Napoleon's objections to such a step; she knew he would argue that, as the ceremony had not already taken place, it was useless to call public attention to its omission, that the greater number of the men who surrounded him were in the same position as himself, and that by setting them such an example he would cause numerous acts of rehabilitation, which would appear to be in opposition to extant civil laws, and would seemingly indicate that the head of the government did not acknowledge the validity of the only mode of marriage which the state recognized, that he would find no lack of reasons to advance for his refusal, any of which might mask a furtive one. Napoleon knew that the Church is accommodating, when she has to deal with the powerful ones of earth, and that when it is advisable she will cut a knot which she had tied, but he felt that if later he was constrained to sunder his marriage relations he would prefer being free to act for himself and not be under obligations to the Holy See.

Josephine divined all this, and was fully alive to the fact that she had nothing to gain by appealing to Napoleon, and had no valid reasons to advance for the religious solemnization of their union; she knew, too, that to assign conscientious scruples as her motive would give not only Napoleon, but the whole court, cause for mirth: but the Pope would not laugh at her.

For several years she had been in correspondence with Pius VII. and quietly paving the way for a religious marriage, so when the Pope called on her at Fontainebleau, she confessed that her union with Bonaparte had not received the sanction of the Church, and the Holy Father, after felicitating her upon her commendable desire to obey the laws of the Church, promised to insist upon the Sacrament. Thus Napoleon's hand was forced, for the Pope was quite capable of postponing the coronation if he postponed the marriage; to refuse to anoint the Emperor, if Napoleon refused to obey the canons of the Church. The ceremony had already been thrice adjourned, and each postponement entailed immense expenditures, gave rise to discontent among the people, and provoked distrust. Paris was filled to overflowing with civil and military deputations, it would have created an awful scandal if the Pope, who had come to Paris solely to anoint and crown the Emperor, returned to Rome without having performed the ceremony; it was absolutely necessary to yield, and on the morning of the 9th December, Cardinal Fesch pronounced the nuptial benediction.

If ever a marriage was forced that one was, and later Napoleon could truthfully affirm that undue influence had been brought to bear upon him, that his consent having been unfairly obtained the marriage was, according to the canons of the Church, null and void; but this Josephine could not foresee, and married by a Cardinal, anointed by a Pope and crowned by the Emperor, she fondly believed her position unassailable.

CHAPTER XI.

MADAME ****.

NAPOLEON would not have been the man he was had he never felt the need of a love not purely animal, of a friendship which should satisfy the sentimental and intellectual side of his nature as well as the physical, and as he advanced in years and his position isolated him more and more from ordinary mortals, the longing for sympathetic companionship grew upon him.

During the early days of the consulate this longing was but faintly felt, but as the fires of youth burned down his intellectual nature assumed the ascendency, and we find ourselves in the presence of a new Napoleon, a man prone to periods of melancholy, possessed by a feverish desire to be understood, and as apt to indulge in dreams of an ideal affection as in ambitious ones, a man delicately tender, who found for the expression of his sentiments language suitable for a hero of romance. As Napoleon has not previously been presented to the world in this light one feels some hesitancy in so doing, but the proofs that his character did thus change, though covering a somewhat later period of his life, are still sufficiently authentic to warrant the assertion.

The women to whom Napoleon addressed himself at this time were no longer actresses and adventuresses, who made capital out of their relations with him, but women of the world who had husbands to deceive and reputations to consider, who were cautious in their indiscretions, destroyed all proof of their relations with the Emperor, and whose descendants carefully guarded the secret, while those who were indiscreet enough to gossip about these ladies took good care to disguise their names; even at this late day he who lifts the light veil which conceals their identity would be most discourteous; moreover, one cannot be *positive* that the veil screens but *one* woman. Naturally one can identify certain traits of person and character, particularly when retaining from childhood a strong and clear impression of a certain face, but such proofs are not documentary, and even at the risk of being obscure and leaving some points unexplained, one must proceed with the greatest caution. There was at the consular court a young woman of twenty, wedded to a man thirty years her senior. The husband was a most respectable person, a great worker, and left the best of reputations behind him ; he was one of those faithful servants of the state of whom the old *régime* made head clerks, and the new, general directors ; he possessed wonderful ability as a financier, and it was he who organized and directed a financial institution which is conducted to-day upon the same lines that he laid down. The wife was charming, graceful and amiable ; her features were irregular, but her face was rendered remarkable by an extremely winning smile and the thoughtful expression of her dark blue eyes—eyes which, it must be admitted, were somewhat deceptive, as they expressed whatever their mistress willed ; her hands and feet were marvellously small and beautiful, she danced like a fairy, sang like an artist, played the harp like a virtuoso, was an excellent listener, and did not display unduly her most remarkable intelligence. This lady lacked neither a strong will, worldly wisdom, ambition nor unscrupulousness, but she concealed her real hardness by a suave manner which enhanced her beauty, and, though of *bourgeoise* origin, she understood the art of politeness better than many a high-born dame, and instinctively comprehended the requirements of good society (a knowledge which must be innate and cannot be acquired) ; and she carried herself with as haughty and disdainful an air as if she had been born in the purple rather than of middle-class provincials. According to certain authorities it was in November, 1803, that Napoleon fell in love with Mme. ****; but the affair with the woman whom Josephine surprised in the orangery at Saint-Cloud seems to destroy this hypothesis, and it is more likely that Napoleon paid his first addresses to Mme. ****, about nine months later, in August, 1804. The child which was born to Mme. **** during that year resembled Bonaparte neither in mind nor feature, a fact which, though it inspired Napoleon with some doubt as to its parentage, was a safeguard to the wife and confirmed her husband's faith in her. It is not uncommon, however, for features as characteristic as those of the Bonapartes to skip one generation and appear, strongly developed, in a second, and it was such a manifestation, occurring a generation later in this family, which revealed a connection which up to that moment had been kept fairly secret. Was the lady at Saint-Cloud the person who, towards the end of the consulate, frequented a little house in the Allée des Veuves where Napoleon also went secretly? Was she the same woman whom Napoleon, disguised and alone, visited by night at her own house in Paris? It is impossible to say. The adventure at

Saint-Cloud seems to have been one of those transitory amours which endure but a day; nocturnal and secret excursions on the part of a man who was ordinarily such a stay-at-home as Napoleon, demonstrate however, an irresistible attraction of which there are few instances in his career. There is some uncertainty regarding the identity of several of the women who played a part in Napoleon's life about that time which, for the moment, it is not advisable to clear up, and about which, memorialists and their editors have been careful not to enlighten us, out of consideration for the woman about whose memory they surge, and above all, for her descendants; nevertheless, there are certain facts regarding which all witnesses agree, and which, though not positive proof, are the strongest sort of circumstantial evidence and permit us to fathom the mystery with which these ladies surround themselves and to divine their names.

A few days before the arrival of the Pope for the coronation, Napoleon, with his whole court, proceeded to Fontainebleau, and his retinue were not slow to perceive that he appeared unusually serene and approachable. One evening, after the Pope had retired to his apartments, the Emperor remained with the Empress, chatting with her ladies-in-waiting; this proceeding did not strike Josephine as natural; her jealousy was awakened, and she began to search for proof of a new intrigue; not knowing exactly whom to suspect, she pounced upon Mme. Ney, who denied emphatically to Hortense, her old schoolfellow at Mme. Campan's, that the Emperor was in any way interested in her, but asserted that he was simply curious about one of the ladies of the court whom Eugène de Beauharnais found quite to his taste. Eugène was but a screen; the lady accepted his attentions and appeared to take pleasure in his society solely to avert suspicion; she was intimate with Caroline Murat, who lent her assistance to the intrigue in order to spite Josephine, as she did in many other instances.

No definite understanding had been arrived at when the court returned to Paris, but Napoleon was captivated by the lady's charms; he was loath to leave the Empress' apartments when she was on duty, and was always ready to join Josephine at the theatre if that lady accompanied her; and, though ordinarily he objected to his wife's going to the play except in state, he was then ready to organize little theatre parties, provided always that Madame *·*** was of the company. Josephine grew more and more uneasy and attempted to remonstrate, but her remonstrances were so ill received that she dared not insist, and although publicly Napoleon seemed more affable and frank than ever before, in reality, unless a certain lady was present, his temper was irritable and uncertain. " Bonaparte makes me a daily and reasonless scene," Josephine wrote a friend about that time; " he is unbearable."

About that time Napoleon was seized with a violent fancy for playing cards in the evening, and invariably called his sister Caroline and two ladies of the palace, one of whom was the object of his affection, to be his partners. He played badly, giving but scant attention to the game, which indeed served only as an excuse for remaining in the society of the woman he so admired, and procured him an opportunity to gaze upon her and to ponder over the charms of an ideal and platonic love; without mentioning names he frequently indulged upon these occasions in long and vehement tirades against jealousy and jealous women ; and poor Josephine, drearily playing whist with court dignitaries, was forced to listen to the invectives which, uttered in his sonorous voice, rang out in the respectful silence of the room and were plainly audible to all.

At a fête given by the minister of war, in honor of the coronation, the women, in accordance with the usage of the day, were alone seated at supper, the Empress with several of her ladies and the wives of state dignitaries occupying the table of honor. Napoleon refused to seat himself but walked about, chatting with various ladies in an unusually gracious and affable manner; he was assiduous in his attentions to Josephine, and taking a plate from the hands of a page served her himself. When he fancied that he had manœuvred enough and had been sufficiently polite to the company in general, he approached Madame * * * * and engaged in conversation with her neighbor, gradually including his charmer, and, perceiving that she wished some olives which were set upon the table at a little distance, he fetched them to her, saying: "You do wrong to eat olives at night, they will make you ill," then, turning to the other lady, he added, " and you, madame, do well not to eat them, above all you are wise not to imitate Madame * * * * for in all things she is inimitable."

The Emperor's stratagem did not impose upon Josephine, whom nothing escaped, and who, in the middle of the winter, had been obliged to yield to a sudden fancy of his and go to Malmaison, a journey which had upset all her plans and made every one excessively uncomfortable, for the visit had been so suddenly undertaken that there had been no time to light the fires, and the first night was spent in a veritable icehouse; the cold, however, had mattered very little to Napoleon who made a nocturnal visit which he flattered himself had been unobserved, little suspecting that Josephine, after a long station behind a glass door, had learned his secret.

After the ministerial fête, the court returned to Malmaison, and the following morning the Empress summoned to her presence the lady who had not partaken of olives, and after an aimless conversation, abruptly asked what the Emperor had said to her on the previous evening, then, what he had said to Madame ****. The lady answered that His Majesty advised Madame **** not to eat olives; "Ah," exclaimed the Empress, "while he was giving her such good advice he might have told her that it is ridiculous for a woman with such a long nose to essay the rôle of Roxelane;" then, taking a book from the chimney-piece, she added: "Here is the book which is turning the heads of all the blonde and thin young women." The volume in question was Mme. de Genlis' novel, "la Duchesse de La Vallière," and the Empress' sarcasm was not idle, for the romance was to be found in the room of every lady-in-waiting; the book had the enormous sale of ten editions, and doubtless the fact that many aspired to a position similar to La Vallière's had not been detrimental to its success.

The Emperor had no intention of installing a

favorite. "I do not wish women to govern in my court," he said upon one occasion, "their influence was harmful to Henri IV and Louis XIV, my mission is more important than theirs was, and the French have become too serious to pardon scandalous *liaisons* of their sovereigns." His real mistress, as he often said, was power, and he had worked too hard to attain it, to permit of its being stolen or even coveted. Madame **** who was both very astute and very intelligently advised, asked nothing for herself, indeed, she was not able to accept many favors, as they might have roused the suspicions of her husband, who was far from being indifferent to his wife's good name and conduct; the most that she was able to secure individually was a position as lady-in-waiting, an appointment which was warranted neither by her position, birth or anything in the past which had endeared her to Bonaparte, and which caused some gossip and many malicious smiles; but little as her relations advantaged her personally, she profited by them to advance the interests of others and her one time protectors became her *protégés*.

Murat, already marshal of the Empire, was promoted to the dignity of a prince and made admiral-in-chief, which classed him, after Cambacérès and Lebrun, among the serene highnesses; but at the same time and of his own accord the Emperor named Eugène de Beauharnais prince and arch-chancellor of state, thus placing him upon the same level as Murat, and establishing the balance between the Bonapartes and the Beauharnais, inclining it even in favor of the Beauharnais. There was a marked difference in the terms which he employed in announcing both decisions to the Senate, and he made the positions which his brother-in-law and his stepson held in his affections most evident; on the one hand it was clear that he yielded to outside pressure and the solicitations of the family, on the other, that he gave freely, actuated by the dictates of his own heart: "In the midst of the anxieties and the bitterness inseparable from the high rank where we are placed, our heart has felt the need of affection and sincere friendship, and its wants have been gratified by this child of our adoption . . . . . our paternal benediction will accompany this young prince throughout his career and, seconded by Providence, he will one day be deserving the approbation of posterity." Such was the speech which announced Eugène de Beauharnais' aggrandizement to the senate; and he had asked for nothing, expressed no dissatisfaction with the position of grand officer of the Empire and colonel of chasseurs which had previously been conferred upon him, as he was on the way to Milan at the head of the mounted guards. It was in truth a fine command, and it was a strange error on the part of Mme. de Rémusat, to represent in the light of a disgrace the greatest favor which the Emperor could bestow upon a general of twenty-three years.

At all events this disgrace, which, according to her, was occasioned by an access of jealousy against Eugène, was of singularly short duration, for he left Paris on the 16th of January in obedience to an order dated on the 14th and which was prompted by the necessity for the appearance of the guards at the coronation at Milan, and it was but fifteen days later that he received a personal letter from the Emperor with a copy of the message to the senate and his nomination as prince and arch-chancellor of state.

Nothing could prove more clearly that Napoleon was drawn closer to Josephine, that he did not propose to be led by any one, and that the affection inspired by Madame * * * * was already on the wane: satiety comes soon when there is no restraint. It was at Malmaison in the heart of winter that the intrigue culminated, and at Malmaison, ere spring-flowers had blossomed, that the chains were broken.

It was while the court was enjoying a fortnight's sojourn at Malmaison, during which Napoleon enjoyed perfect freedom, and could walk, talk and enjoy the society of Madame * * * * to his heart's content, while Josephine mourned and pined in the seclusion of her chamber, that the final rupture occurred. One morning the Emperor went to his wife's apartments and returning to his old confidential manner, admitted that he had been very much in love but was disillusioned, and finished by asking Josephine to aid him to sunder his relations with Madame * * * * The Empress took the matter in hand and summoned the lady, who, perfectly mistress of herself, did not manifest the slightest emotion and opposed to the Empress' remarks a mute disdain and a face as impassive as marble.

Although the Emperor never renewed his allegiance, Madame * * * * always remained tenderly attached to him, while he invariably manifested for her the greatest consideration, according her every favor compatible with her husband's position, and designating her among the first for court honors and favors. During his hours of trial she was one of his most faithful adherents, she enhanced the fêtes of the hundred days with her beauty, and when, after Waterloo, the vanquished hero was about to leave his country forever, Madame * * * * was one of the last to visit Malmaison and offer to the dethroned Emperor the tribute of her respectful attachment and unalterable devotion.

CHAPTER XII.

STEPHANIE DE BEAUHARNAIS.

PRIOR even to Austerlitz, Napoleon resolved to establish family relations between his house and the sovereign houses of Europe which would serve to consolidate political alliances; he was of the opinion that his government would never be firmly established in Europe until the blood of the Napoleons mingled with that of older reigning families, and not believing himself marriageable, he mobilized around him all who were, boys and girls, with the view of strengthening the only bond to which he attached any value, because he did not think it subject to political hazards. From his point of view nothing was more binding, even to princes, than ties of blood.

His first step, on returning from the campaign, was to arrange a marriage between Eugène de Beauharnais and the Princess Augusta of Bavaria; she was betrothed to the Prince of Baden, but that was of no importance, Napoleon finding another wife for the discarded lover in the person of Stéphanie-Louise-Adrienne de Beauharnais, the daughter of Claude de Beauharnais, Count of Roches-Baritaud, and of Adrienne de Lezay-Marnésia his first wife, and cousin, sixteen degrees removed, to Hortense and Eugène.

Stéphanie de Beauharnais was born at Paris on the 26th of August, 1789, and, losing her mother at the age of four years, spent some time in the convent of Panthémont; a certain Lady de Bath, an old friend of her mother's, then took the young girl under her protection and, when the convents were closed, confided her ward to two of the sisters, Mmes. de Trélissac and de Sabatier, who took Stéphanie with them, first to Castelsarrasin, then to Périgueux and later to Montauban. Her paternal grandmother, Fanny de Beauharnais, occupied herself at Cubières with poetry and flirtations, her father was an *émigré*, and her grandfather, Marquis de Marnésia, was travelling in America, so that, save for the kindness of Lady de Bath, the child would have been left to public charity. One day, in the beginning of the consulate, Josephine happened to speak of her little cousin before her husband, and Bonaparte, who thought so much of ties of blood, was indignant at his wife for leaving one of her name to the care of a stranger and an Englishwoman. He immediately sent for the child, but the nuns refused to deliver her to the messenger, whereupon he sent a courier armed with legal authority to take Stéphanie de Beauharnais, and the sisters were forced to obey, though not without tears and grave misgivings. Upon her arrival in Paris the child was placed with Mme. Campan, and thenceforth she was one of the little group of young girls who came to Malmaison each *décadi* (the republican day of rest), and whose white-robed forms and cheery laughter enlivened the park as they flitted about under the shade of the great chestnut trees. Both Josephine and Hortense were extremely kind to Stéphanie, but she did not appear on gala days, had no rank, was of no importance, and seemed destined to such a marriage as had been arranged for her cousin Emilie de Beauharnais, Mme. Lavallette; the little lady, however, did not take that view of the situation, but assumed the airs of a princess and treated those of her relations who were not honored with a lodging in the imperial palace very haughtily.

Such was the situation when Eugène married and it became necessary to provide a wife for the Prince of Baden; Napoleon first thought of another ward of Josephine's, her niece, Stéphanie Tascher, but afterwards decided upon Stéphanie de Beauharnais, and the arrangements for the marriage were definitely concluded by him while on his way to Carlsruhe, on the 20th of January, 1806, and were confirmed by an agreement signed at Paris on the 17th of February.

Stéphanie was at that time seventeen years of age, was clever, bright and gay, with a certain childishness of manner which was very taking ; she had rather a pretty face, a fine complexion, sparkling blue eyes and beautiful blonde hair. Upon the Emperor's return to Paris she was taken from her boarding-school to the Tuileries and installed in an apartment near that of the Empress and became at once the life of the palace ; gay, piquant and agreeable, she enlivened the dreary salons, and not being in the least embarrassed by the Emperor she indulged her mischievousness as freely in his presence as elsewhere, which greatly pleased and amused him ; she was not long in perceiving this and increased her efforts to divert him, and they were soon engaged in a lively flirtation. Possibly Napoleon hoped for something more, but Mlle. de Beauharnais was not so inclined ; she only wished for distraction and to make the most of Napoleon's friendship and admiration without compromising herself ; she was well aware that it was not because she was Mlle. de Beauharnais that she was to espouse the Prince of Baden, but because she was a Napoleonite, that the manner of her reception by the prince's family depended entirely upon the Emperor, and that it was therefore prudent to find out how much he would do for her.

Stéphanie's struggle was not with the Empress, but with the sisters of Napoleon, who had no intention of yielding her precedence, and who, Caroline Murat particularly, snubbed her mercilessly, but little Stéphanie made light of their rudeness and laughed gayly at everything until Caroline, exasperated, became insolent. One evening, while they were waiting for the Emperor, Stéphanie seated herself on a folding chair, upon which the Princess Caroline ordered her to rise, saying, that it was not customary for young persons to remain seated in the presence of the Emperor's sisters; Stéphanie rose immediately, but she no longer laughed, on the contrary, she wept bitterly; the Emperor, entering at that moment, perceived her tears, and inquired their source. "Is that all!" he exclaimed when Stéphanie told her grievance, "well, come and sit on my knee, and you won't incommode anybody!"

This anecdote is lent an appearance of authenticity by a note which is found upon the register of the master of ceremonies: "Our will is, that the Princess Stéphanie-Napoleon, our daughter, shall in all circles enjoy all the privileges due her rank, and that at fêtes and at table she shall be seated at our side, and in case we are not present that she shall be placed at the Empress' right hand." This gave Stéphanie precedence over the Emperor's sisters, sisters-in-law, Hortense, and even over the Princess Augusta of Bavaria.

On the following day a message announced to the senate the adoption of Stéphanie de Beauharnais and her approaching marriage with the Prince of Baden, and ordered the State to send a deputation to pay her respects, in which ceremony M. Claude de Beauharnais, the princess's own father, figured conspicuously.

M. de Beauharnais, on his return from exile, had entered the senate, and was then a member of some years' standing, with a salary of twenty-five thousand francs a year, and he was about to enjoy the benefits accruing from the parentage of a charming daughter. Napoleon appointed him to the senatorship of Amiens, which brought him an income of twenty-five thousand francs; in 1807 endowed him with twenty-five thousand eight hundred and eighty-two francs, and in 1810 made him chevalier d' honneur to Marie-Louise, a position which commanded a salary of thirty thousand francs, and on the 22d of September, 1807, made him a personal present of two hundred thousand francs; but all this was a mere bagatelle in comparison with what the Emperor did for Stéphanie. He took a personal interest in her trousseau, ordering for her a tulle dress covered with an embroidery of gold thread and interwoven with precious stones, the cost of which was twenty-four thousand francs; from Lenormand he commanded twelve dresses, at prices ranging from nineteen hundred to twelve hundred francs; from Leroy he commanded forty-five thousand, one hundred and seventy-eight francs and ninety-six centimes' worth of millinery and trinkets, and from Roux-Montagnat, two thousand, five hundred and seventy-four francs' worth of artificial flowers; in addition to all this he gave her a dot of fifteen hundred thousand francs, a superb *parure* of diamonds, and presented her with a thousand *louis* from his private purse.

Both the civil and religious marriages were celebrated with the utmost pomp and magnificence; Napoleon could not have done more for his own child, and the festivities were not confined to the palace, but overflowed into the city, which was illuminated by fireworks set off on the Place de la Concorde. When the last spark had died, the last note of the band had sounded, and the guests had departed, the Emperor and Empress, according to usage, conducted the bride and groom to the bridal chamber, but it was found impossible to induce

Stéphanie to occupy it; she wept and sobbed, and insisted that her school-fellow, Mlle. Nelly Bourjolly, should sleep with her. The court went to Malmaison on the following day, but Stéphanie, in spite of all the arguments brought to bear upon her, still remained obdurate. Some one told the prince that his wife's repugnance arose from the manner in which he dressed his hair, as she detested a cue, thereupon he had his hair cut short; but as soon as Stéphanie perceived him she burst out laughing and declared that he was uglier than before. Night after night the prince went to her door, supplicating and praying for admittance, and at last exhausted threw himself upon a couch in the antechamber and fell asleep; in the morning he went and complained to the Empress, while Napoleon smilingly watched the couple who naturally were the talk of the château.

That this state of affairs gave the Emperor a certain amount of satisfaction, that he bore Stéphanie no ill-will was proved by the superb fête which he gave at the Tuileries in honor of her marriage: the first great ball to which not only the court but the gentry of the city were bidden. Nothing equalling the two quadrilles—one in the gallery of Diana conducted by the Princess Louise, the other in the *Salle des Maréchaux*, conducted by the Princess Caroline—had ever been seen, while the lavishness of the refreshments set all the world talking: there were sixty *entrées*, sixty roasts and two hundred desserts; one thousand bottles of Beaune, one hundred of Champagne, one hundred of Bordeaux and one hundred of sweet wines were consumed; but the festivities did not soften Stéphanie's heart.

Political reasons intervening, Napoleon saw himself obliged to interfere. Mlle. de Beauharnais' coqueteries had amused him and supplied a pretext for teasing his wife, but he had permitted himself rather too much latitude in according to the young girl a rank disproportionate to her birth and fortune and in celebrating her marriage in princely style; he now saw that the patience of the ruler of Baden was nearly exhausted, and, as a war with Prussia was imminent, felt it expedient to conciliate all the German princes who might become auxiliaries, or at least give valuable information.

Having respected Stéphanie previous to her marriage, he did not afterwards meditate making her his mistress, and the flirtation which was suitable neither to his dignity, his age nor his temperament, grew wearisome, and it was becoming embarrassing to have her longer at Paris, while she might be of service at Carlsruhe, if only in counterbalancing the hostile influence of Markgraf Louis and the little German court.

Napoleon hardly took time to investigate the little stories contained in certain intercepted letters, which proved only too plainly what an inhospitable reception awaited his adopted daughter, but hastened her departure. Stéphanie left France despairing; she took with her three of her school-friends: Mlles. de Mackau, Bourjolly and Gruau, and as soon as she arrived in her father-in-law's principality, she wrote to the Emperor: "Sire, each day when I am at liberty I think of you and the Empress, of all who are dearest to me; in imagination, I am in France and near you, and I find a certain pleasure in my sadness." Napoleon responded rather severely, without making use of any paternal or tender expressions. "Carlsruhe," he wrote, "is a charming place of residence. Make yourself agreeable to the Elector, who is now your father, and love your husband, who merits your affection by the tenderness he lavishes upon you." When she had answered in a manner which pleased him, saying that she was contented at Carlsruhe, Napoleon wrote more kindly, calling her *daughter*, but recommending the same line of conduct; and he did not become thoroughly amiable until the hereditary grand duke asked him to make the campaign with him, and in the same letter announced that Stéphanie was about to become a mother ; then he wrote, saying : "I only hear good news of you and hope you will continue to be kind and gentle to all who surround you ; " he then authorized her to rejoin the Empress and Hortense at Mayence, and to remain with them while her husband was with the army, and thereafter, to all his letters to Josephine he added a kindly message for Stéphanie. In 1807, Stéphanie and her husband were invited to Paris on the occasion of the marriage of Jérôme Bonaparte with Catherine of Wurtemberg, and she hastened to accept ; but if she retained any illusion concerning the Emperor's affection and the exceptional rank which only a year previous he had bestowed upon her, she must have been cruelly disappointed, for the place assigned her was the very last among the princesses, and it was only by courtesy that she took a place in the Imperial family ; by favor that she was given a folding-chair when the family were seated. She had become a princess of the German confederation, and had there been any of the reigning German princesses present, they would have taken precedence over her. At first Stéphanie did not seem to perceive her downfall, and took pleasure in flirting with Jérôme, the new King of Westphalia, but her aunt remarking upon her conduct, the situation became clear, and realizing that she could only hold her position through her husband, she managed to inspire him with so much affection that he became unsupportably jealous.

Did the prince stand by Stéphanie in 1814, when, after the Emperor's downfall, he was urged to repudiate her and turn out of the palace of Zaehringen this unwelcome witness to broken oaths, whose presence constantly recalled favors whose authors the reigning house of Baden desired to forget? Was it because of his fidelity that at the age of thirty-two, this man, previously in the most vigorous health, fell suddenly ill, and after dragging for a year died of a strange malady in 1818? Stéphanie, although the mother of numerous children, was unable to preserve one son; when she lost the second, or believed him dead, she wrote broken-heartedly to the Emperor: "I was so happy to tell your Majesty that I had a son and to beseech your protection for him. A son made me forget my griefs and was necessary to my position which is often a difficult one—now I have lost my only hope!" She grieved unceasingly over the fatality which followed her sons and took from her race, stricken because of her with political sterility, the heredity of the throne of Baden.

Ten years after the death of the grand duke, between four and five o'clock on the morning of the 26th of May, 1828, a *bourgeois* met a young man of seventeen, who muttered only one or two phrases in low German in the Tallow Market of Nuremberg; the youth had never walked, his eyes had never seen the sun's light, his stomach was unable to support animal food, but he would never have been thus deformed had he not since babyhood been sequestered in solitude and obscurity. Stéphanie was the first to ponder, calculate, and be convinced that the mysterious and unknown youth at Nurenberg, who was called Kaspar Hauser, was her own son—her child, in whose place a dead baby had been substituted, and who, a victim to the hatred of Markgraf Louis, and the ambition of Countess Hochberg, had for nearly sixteen years expiated in darkness and solitude the sin of having a Napoleonite for his mother. Poor Stéphanie was unable to do anything, for her enemies were triumphant and powerful; one reigned upon the throne of Baden, and she could tremble for Kaspar Hauser, and weep over his sad fate, when, after escaping three ambuscades, he was finally assassinated.

Was hers one of those illusions with which a mother loves to comfort her heart, or one of those revelations, which, better than all the investigations of justice, sometimes throw light upon a great crime? However this may be, Stéphanie firmly believed to her last hour (she died on the 29th of January, 1860), that Kaspar Hauser was her lost son, and to the few friends whom she received in the tumble-down palace of Mannheim, she asserted that her son did not die in 1812, but that he had been stolen from her, designating the authors and accomplices in the crime. Some German authors have attempted to demonstrate that the poor mother deceived herself; for the credit of the reigning house of Baden, it is to be hoped she did.

CHAPTER XIII.

ELEONORE.

TOWARDS the close of the revolution, Mme. Campan, once a confidential member of Marie Antoinette's household, established a school for young ladies at Saint-Germain-en-Laye ; Josephine became the patroness of the institution, and there her daughter and nieces were educated. This group of young girls, so closely allied to the imperial family, drew around them the daughters of those who had, or sought for, some appointment under the Consulate, and Mme. Campan's nieces making excellent marriages, thanks to their intimacy with Hortense, the school was still further augmented by the daughters of intriguing parents who hoped their children might also profit by the acquaintance of their royal school-fellows.

Mme. Campan was supposedly an influential person, having obtained positions for numerous people, pardons for exiles and the restitution of confiscated property ; her school was the fashionable one of the day, and on the list of pupils can be seen, side by side with names of people who had recently attained eminence, the old historical ones of Noailles, Talon, Lally-Tollendal, and Rochemond.

After the Consulate, the reputation of the school diminished somewhat, and among the scholars there was a young girl of whose origin Mme. Campan was somewhat in ignorance, and who could probably never have been a pupil had the principal then been as strict regarding the parentage of those whom she admitted as she was in the days of the school's great popularity. This young lady was Mlle. Louise-Catherine-Eléonore Dénuelle de La Plaigne. The father claimed to be a man of wealth, but his business ventures were not always successful; the mother, who was still very pretty, was rather gay, and the family lived in a sumptuous apartment on the Boulevard des Italiens, received a great deal of rather mixed company, and managed as best they could from day to day, awaiting the time when their daughter should make a rich marriage.

Time passed, Mme. Dénuelle aged, the father ran into debt, the quarterly tuition was hard to pay, and, moreover, since the departure of the Beauharnais from Mme. Campan's, the chances of meeting a desirable *partie* in that establishment, had greatly diminished; so, as Mme. Dénuelle had not access to salons where her daughter might have made such acquaintances, she determined to show her at the theatres. One evening at the Gaîté, a good-looking officer entered the box where Mme Dénuelle and her daughter occupied seats, and took the vacant place; the ladies were not haughty, the officer was gallant, and an acquaintance grew apace.

Mme. Dénuelle invited the young man to visit them and he did not fail to do so; he soon became so enamored of Eléonore as to ask her hand in marriage, and the wedding took place on the fifteenth of January, 1805, at Saint-Germain.

This officer, Jean-Honoré-François Revel, who claimed to be a captain of the 15th regiment of dragoons and the aide-de-camp of General d'Avrange d'Haugeranville, was a knave. He had resigned from the regiment of which he was once quartermaster, and claimed that he expected to get a contract for supplying the army with provisions; in the meanwhile he lived on credit. He appears to have counted more upon the beauty of his young wife to extricate him from his embarrassment than upon any efforts of his own, and two months after the wedding he was arrested and imprisoned for attempting to pass a forged check.

Eléonore then bethought herself that the Princess

Caroline Murat had been her school-fellow, and, warmly recommended by Mme. Campan, solicited her highness' protection. The princess first placed her in a sort of asylum at Chantilly, where unfortunate women like herself were received; later, in despite of Mme. Campan's advice, she yielded to Eléonore's solicitations and installed her in her own household.

Mme. Revel was an extremely handsome brunette, tall and graceful, with large, dark eyes and a lively, coquettish manner; she had not been educated to entertain scruples, and she certainly had not acquired any in the two months she spent with Revel. At first her duty was to announce the princess' guests, later she was promoted to the dignity of reader, and when, after the Emperor's return from Austerlitz towards the end of January, 1806, he came to visit his sister, Mme. Eléonore deftly managed to make herself noticeable and as soon as propositions were made to her accepted with enthusiasm, and allowed herself to be conducted to the Tuileries; from thenceforth she went there habitually, spending two or three hours in the Emperor's society.

Revel had been condemned by the criminal court to two years' imprisonment, and on the 13th of April his wife asked for a divorce, which was granted on the 29th of April, 1806; it was high time, for on the 13th of December, 1806, at No. 29 rue de la Victoire, she was delivered of a male child who was registered as "Léon, son of Mlle. Dénuelle, property-holder, aged twenty, and of an absent father."

There was no doubt as to the child's parentage; Eléonore who in her prayer for divorce had stated that she was "attached to the person of Mme. la Princess Caroline," had, from the time she returned from Chantilly, lived in a small house in the rue de Provence, which she never left save for her visits to the Tuileries—visits of which Caroline knew the secret—moreover, the child's resemblance to Napoleon was so striking as to confute doubt. Thus the event which Josephine so dreaded came to pass; the charm was broken, for henceforth the Emperor entertained no doubts regarding his ability to provide an heir to the throne.

The Emperor was at Pulstuck, when, on the 31st of December, the news of Eléonore's *accouchement* reached him, and doubtless the birth of this illegitimate son was strongly instrumental in the formation of plans which two years later he carried into execution.

The child Léon was at first confided to the care of Mme. Loir, foster-mother of Achille Murat; later, in 1812, M. Mathieu de Mauvières, mayor of the commune of Saint-Forget, baron of the Empire and father-in-law of Méneval, the Emperor's private secretary, was appointed guardian to the boy, and an independent fortune was settled upon him by his imperial father. Not content with this, in January, 1814, when about to leave Paris to join the army, Napoleon authorized the Duke de Bassano to add twelve thousand pounds income, and to this, on the 21st of June, 1815, was added canal stock valued at one hundred thousand francs, and finally, actuated by conscience, the Emperor added a codicil to his will in which he bequeathed to Léon three hundred and twenty thousand francs for the purchase of a country seat, and as long as he lived interested himself in his son's welfare. The thirty-seventh paragraph of his testamentary instructions to his executors, proves that the lad was never forgotten : "If his taste runs in that direction," wrote Napoleon, "I should be pleased to have little Léon enter the magistracy."

To avoid a rupture with Josephine, to whom he was still sincerely attached, and at the same time to comply with the law of heredity in a manner which seemed to him both satisfactory and natural, Napoleon conceived the idea of adopting his natural son, spoke of it to the Empress, sounded many of his confidants on the subject, and invoked precedents to justify his inclination. That he did not carry these plans into execution is probably due to the fact that he realized that the days of Louis XIV. were past, and that the country would not permit him to follow the example given by that monarch, who had designated the Duke de Maine and the Comte de Toulouse as his heirs to the throne.

Napoleon became very much attached to this child, and frequently had him brought either to the Élysée or to his sister Caroline's, sometimes received him even at the Tuileries while dressing or at breakfast; he played with him, gave him dainties to eat and was amused by Léon's childish chatter. As time passed Napoleon was necessarily unable to bestow the same personal attention upon Léon, but in 1815 he recommended the boy to the care of his mother and Cardinal Fesch. Mme. Bonaparte was already interested in the boy and seemed disposed to do a great deal for him, but unfortunately Léon's was not a character to inspire warm affection.

In 1832—he was then twenty-five—Dénuelle was already nearly ruined, owing to his passion for gambling, and applied for assistance to Cardinal Fesch, swearing that he would never again lose forty-five thousand francs at a sitting. It was a gambler's oath, for a year later he was as badly off as ever, attempting to brazen out his affairs, mixing with visionary politicians and engaging right and left in duels, for he was brave and somewhat of a bully. In 1834, by trading on the name of the grand man to whom he owed his existence, he was elected chief of the communal battalion of the national guards of Saint-Denis; he was soon suspended for disobedience to orders, but afterwards reinstated, and attempted to justify himself by the publication of a number of pamphlets, which are, however, so hazy that they could hardly have served to clear his character before the public. In 1840 he was one of the official cortége on the return from Cendres, and, being absolutely ruined, began a series of lawsuits against his mother with the intention of wringing money from her, she having preserved her fortune intact.

The Emperor had never renewed his relations with Léon's mother, had, indeed, refused to receive her when, in 1807, she presented herself at Fontainebleau, but he acquitted his debt to her by giving her a house in the rue de la Victoire, and a dot of twenty-two thousand pounds, which was not transferable. She married, in 1808, a lieutenant of infantry, M. Pierre-Philippe Augier, who took her to Spain with him, and who died in captivity after the Russian campaign. Eléonore was not inconsolable, for at

Seckenheim, on the 25th of May, 1814, she was married for the third time to M. Charles-Auguste-Emile, Count de Luxbourg, and a major in the service of the king of Bavaria. Returning to Paris with her third husband she was obliged to combat the first, for Revel, profiting by the fall of Napoleon, posed as a victim and essayed to blackmail his ex-wife ; Mme. de Luxbourg resisted, and Revel, to avenge himself and to make a few pennies, published innumerable pamphlets whose titles were startling, and admirably combined to attract attention and create a scandal, but he was defeated in everything he attempted against his former wife. Léon was somewhat more fortunate in his suits against his mother, for, although he lost a suit wherein he charged her with swindling and attempted to force her to render an account of her income, he succeeded in having himself acknowledged as her natural son, and on the second of July, 1846, he obtained a lump sum of four thousand francs instead of the yearly allowance which he had sued for. In 1848 he seems to have been somewhat better off financially, for he meditated persenting himself as a candidate for the presidency of the Republic in competition with the Prince Louis Napoleon, with whom, eight years previous, in March, 1840, he had been ambitious to fight a duel. Léon's conduct in this respect was so singular that it can only be explained by the supposition that he was mentally deranged. In 1848 he put forth his claims in a manifesto beginning: "Citizen Léon, ex-count Léon, son of the Emperor Napoleon, director of the Pacific Society, to the French people."

The empire re-installed, Dénuelle obtained from Napoleon III. a pension of six thousand francs, and the payment of Napoleon's first legacy to him of two hundred and twenty-five thousand, three hundred and nineteen francs, but that did not content him, and in 1853 he reclaimed five hundred and seventy-two thousand, six hundred and seventy francs in virtue of some visionary decree, and in 1857 sued the minister of Public Works for the sum of five hundred thousand francs, which he claimed was due him for draughts made by him for the *chemin de fer du Nord*. Not a year passed that he did not bring forward some claim or petition, and the civil list paid his debts five or six times; but he was irrepressible and his brain was in a state of perpetual evolution up to the time of his death, which occurred at Pontoise on the 15th of April, 1881.

HORTENSE.

CHAPTER XIV.

HORTENSE.

THE year 1807 was a decisive one in the life of Napoleon; the month of January being marked by the birth of Léon, which gave to him the certitude that he could have a direct heir, and May by the death of Napoleon-Charles, eldest son of Louis and Hortense. With him died Napoleon's dream of creating an heredity by adoption, and the child's death was also a sad blow to his affections. Napoleon-Charles had been doubly dear to the Emperor, being the son of the girl, who, from the moment he met her, had taken such a hold upon his heart that he had accorded to her tears the pardon refused her mother, and to whom he had been both father and guardian. Napoleon-Charles was the child also of his best-loved brother, "the little brother" who had been to him almost as a son, whom he had lodged, fed and educated when he had but a lieutenant's scanty pay; whom he had made his aide-de-camp and the witness of his victories, whom he had ennobled as he himself rose in rank, until he stood close to the throne. In his nephew Napoleon saw all the characteristics of the Bonapartes, undisfigured by Louis' blobber-lip and ugly nose, and unbeautified by the slender grace of his mother's family, but a Bonaparte through and through, idealized only by an aureole of golden hair. To this child, the first male of his generation, Napoleon had given his father's name, and he had shown such a lively affection for the boy that gossips had begun by insinuating, and had finally asserted, that he was the child's real father, that his step-daughter had been his mistress before becoming Louis' wife.

Hortense's marriage-contract was signed on the 3d of January, 1802, the marriage celebrated on the 4th, and her son was born on the 10th of October, 1802, therefore she was certainly not *enceinte* when she married, since there were two hundred and eighty days between the time she was wed and the birth of her child.

Louis Bonaparte was the most jealous and suspicious of husbands; he tyrannized over his wife from the hour of their marriage; he never left her, had her constantly under surveillance, and forbade her to pass even one night at Saint-Cloud. Suffering from an illness due to youthful indiscretions, he at first essayed to effect a cure by taking tripe baths, the stench of which infected the old orangery which stood at the end of the Terrasse des Feuillant; later, to draw out the humor, he slept in the night-gown and sheets which had previously served a hospital patient afflicted with the itch, and he obliged his wife to sleep on a little bed in the same room with him. Every maid who showed the slightest affection for Hortense was pitilessly discharged; his mother-in-law was a target for the gravest accusations, yet Louis had never the slightest doubt of his wife's virtue. In his "*Documents Historiques sur la Hollande,*" he affirms that he was the father of the three children whom his wife and he "loved with equal tenderness;" this affirmation he repeated both in prose and in verse, for he thought himself a poet; and when, on the Emperor's proposal to adopt Napoleon-Charles, Louis alluded to the current reports regarding the boy's paternity, it was not because he attached the slightest importance to them, but because they served as a pretext for not yielding to his brother's wishes. Louis-Napoleon had an unfortunately melancholy and peculiar disposition, but he loved his son as much as he could love any one, and the child's death was a severe trial; after this loss he was for a time reconciled to Hortense, with whom he previously lived so unhappily that his imperial brother had more than once seen fit to remonstrate with him, and he wrote kind and affectionate letters to Josephine, whom ordinarily he detested. Shortly after the death of her son, Hortense, who was in poor health, went to Cauterets accompanied by her husband, and it was there, under circumstances the details of which are well-known, that she became *enceinte* with her third son, Charles-Louis-Napoleon, afterwards known as Napoleon III.; thus Louis Bonaparte never believed for an instant that Hortense had been his brother's mistress, and not only did he bear witness to his faith in her virtue, but his conduct was an affirmation of his convictions; as for Hortense, until 1809, she remained ignorant that such gossip was afloat.

Josephine's marriage with General Bonaparte had wounded her daughter to the quick, for she felt it to be almost a crime for her mother to wed one who was a soldier under the Republic, a man whose political principles were similar to those entertained by the men who had caused her father's execution. Previous to her mother's marriage, Hortense lived at Saint-Germain-en-Laye, near her grandfather, the Marquis de Beauharnais and her aunt, Mme. Rénaudin, whom he had recently married. At the beginning of the Consulate she was entered at Mme. Campan's, and she did not go to live at the Tuileries until about the time when the Consul left

France for Marengo; thus it was not until Bonaparte returned from Italy that Hortense saw him continually and familiarly.

Napoleon always entertained a tender and paternal affection for his wife's daughter, which she returned only with timid respect; she trembled when addressing him, dared ask nothing of him, and when obliged to make a request employed intermediaries. "The little goose," Napoleon frequently said, "why don't she speak to me; why is the child so afraid of me?" He did not interfere when Josephine arranged the marriage between her daughter and Louis Bonaparte, because he hoped that this marriage might unite his own family and that of his wife, and foresaw that it might be politically judicious, and he also felt a delicacy in interfering with any of Josephine's plans for her children; but whenever he thought it necessary he did not hesitate to counsel Louis as to his conduct towards Hortense, and with the most admirable tact and delicacy strove to calm his jealous fears and point out to him wherein his conduct was faulty. He pitied his step-daughter, venerated her, and guarded his speech in her presence; on more than one occasion he said: "Hortense obliges me to believe in virtue."

Napoleon was not ignorant of the rumors which

were afloat regarding his relations with his stepdaughter, rumors which some of those who were very near to him were assiduous in spreading and which were amplified by the English papers. In order to put a stop to the calumnies he bethought himself of a plan which does greater credit to his knightly intentions than to his discrimination; he commanded a ball to be given at Malmaison, and that Hortense, although then in her seventh month, should assist at it; he invited her to dance, but Hortense declined, alleging that she was weary, although in reality her refusal arose from her knowledge of her stepfather's dislike of seeing women who were *enceinte* upon the floor of a ballroom, above all, when, as was the fashion of the time, they were clothed in such clinging garments that the outlines of the figure were plainly discernible. The Emperor, however, insisted, asking simply for a contredance, and, after persisting for some time in her refusal, she finally yielded. The following morning a newspaper published some gallant verses upon the subject, and Hortense, furious, complained to the Emperor, but received no satisfaction; the truth being that the ball had been given solely to furnish occasion for the verses, and so force the public to acknowledge that she was not so far advanced in pregnancy as was currently reported;

it was with this view also that the *Moniteur*, which up to that time had never spoken of the Consul's family, inserted in its edition of October 12th, 1802, the following announcement: "On the 10th inst., at 9 o'clock in the evening, a son was born to Monsieur and Madame Louis Bonaparte."

Napoleon did all in his power to crush the calumny, but his efforts proved unavailing; so he gradually accustomed himself to look upon the report from a political standpoint and cogitated how he might turn it to account. He felt an almost paternal affection for Napoleon-Charles, and some of the happiest hours of his life were spent in play with him; it delighted him to hear the child cry: "Long live Nanon the soldier!" when he saw a grenadier pass, and he frequently had the little fellow sit by his side while he dined, being highly amused by the child's desire to touch everything and by the agility with which he seized and upset everything within reach of his baby hands. The Emperor frequently took Napoleon-Charles to the garden to feed tobacco to the gazelles, and, seating him astride one of them, would roar with laughter at the baby's antics; he often sent for the child when in his dressing-room, and, after caressing him and making the most extraordinary grimaces for his amusement, would end by sitting down upon the floor, the better to play with him. Napoleon loved the little nephew, whom the people claimed was his own son, as though he were verily bone of his bone and flesh of his flesh, and therefore the idea of adopting him as his heir was not repugnant, even if by so doing the people were convinced of the truth of their suppositions. In this lad he believed they would find impersonated the characteristics of his race and his own genius, and that they could not claim that the line which he had founded was built upon a fiction. It must be admitted that this plan was contrary to all established ideas, but Napoleon had no prejudices and believed that his exceptional destiny placed him above humanity at large, that the nation would not judge him according to accepted moral formulas, and that the people's desire to assure the stability of his government would cause them to overlook the unconventionality of the proceeding, the more easily as they could not confirm the existing suspicion.

It must not be supposed that it is upon simple supposition only that we accredit the Emperor with these ideas and projects; we base our statements upon a conversation which he had with Hortense, two years after the death of her son, and which is related at length in her unpublished *mémoires*. He then spoke freely to his step-daughter regarding the consequences attendant upon the death of Napoleon-Charles, who, as he said, was thought to be his son as well as hers. "You know," Napoleon said, "how absurd such a supposition is, but you could not convince all Europe that the child was not mine," he stopped a moment, arrested by a movement of surprise from Hortense, then continued: "Your reputation does not suffer on this account, as you are generally esteemed; nevertheless, the idea receives credence everywhere; it was perhaps best that it was so, and for that reason I regard his death as a great misfortune." "I was so surprised," wrote Hortense, "that I was unable to utter a word, I no longer heard what he said. That reflection, *it was perhaps best that it was believed,*' tore a veil from before my eyes and pierced me to the heart; was it possible that he who had been so kind and generous, in whom I seemed to find my own lost father, had been actuated throughout by political motives and not by affection!"

Hortense was mistaken, for if Napoleon had been actuated by policy he also was moved by affection, but her indignation was quite natural, considering that she looked upon the situation from a woman's point of view, and was unable to conceive of the profound subtlety of Napoleon's reasoning. If he had showered kindnesses and attentions upon Hortense it had not been in order to confirm the story that Napoleon-Charles was his son, on the contrary he had made every effort to refute it; but the gossip persisting and a conviction of its truth being firmly established in the public mind he had sought to utilize it for his own interests and the consolidation of his dynasty; it was a battlefield inspiration which he had had, for one of his most remarkable faculties was the ability to look situations clearly in the face, to discern at a glance precisely where he stood, make the best of affairs, and act promptly upon his intuitions.

It was owing to his belief in a philosophical acceptance of all situations, that, while he felt keenly the loss of Napoleon-Charles, he accepted the inevitable with calmness. The remark, "I have not time to indulge in sentimental regrets like other men," has been accredited him; it might better be admitted that the death of his poor little nephew was a grief to him, for he wrote to all his correspondents, at least twenty times to Josephine, six or seven to Hortense, and severally to Joseph, Jérôme, Fouché and Monge, expressing his sorrow, but adding, "that it was destiny." It was not in Napoleon's nature, nor in accordance with the philosophical formula which the continual spectacle of war and death in all its most terrible forms had imposed upon his spirit, to yield to idle tears when a destiny was accomplished.

Napoleon-Charles was one of the ties which attached Bonaparte to Josephine, and this tie broken there only remained between them those bonds of tenderness which were woven by ten years of wedded life; years broken by long absences, marred by frequent quarrels and strange misunderstandings. Could these bonds resist such a strain as they were subjected to in 1805 by his *liaison* with Madame * * * * ?

CHAPTER XV.

MADAME WALEWSKA.

On the 1st of January, 1807, the Emperor, on his way from Pulstuck to Warsaw, stopped to change post-horses at the little town of Bronie ; a noisy and enthusiastic crowd awaited the liberator of Poland, and rushed to surround the imperial carriage as soon as it came in sight. As the carriage stopped before the post-house, General Duroc descended and cleared an entrance ; he was about to pass the door when he heard a cry of entreaty, saw hands lifted in supplication, and a voice addressing him in French, said : "Oh, sir, pray get us out of this crowd, and arrange so that I may obtain even a glimpse of His Majesty !" Duroc paused and looking about saw that the demand came from two ladies, who seemed sadly out of place in the multitude of peasants and workmen ; the one who spoke to him seemed almost a child, she was very fair and fragile, with great, blue, innocent-looking eyes which at that moment glowed with patriotic enthusiasm ;

her skin, of the texture and freshness of a tea-rose, was flushed with embarrassment, and her slender yet supple and graceful form trembled with excitement; she was dressed very simply, and wore a dark hat wound about with a black veil.

Duroc took in the situation at a glance, and extricating the two ladies from the crowd gave his hand to the blonde and led her to the carriage door. "Sire," he said to Napoleon, "deign to greet these ladies, who braved the dangers of the crowd to see you."

The Emperor lifted his hat and leaning towards the lady began to talk to her, but she, as she afterwards recounted, was so excited by the emotions which agitated her that she did not permit him to finish his sentence. "Welcome, Sire," she exclaimed, "a thousand times welcome to Poland! Nothing which we can do can sufficiently demonstrate the affection we bear you, nor the pleasure we Poles feel in having you step upon this land which looks to you for deliverance."

While the lady spoke, Napoleon watched her closely, and when she ceased, took a bouquet from the carriage, presented it to her and said: "Keep this as a guarantee of my good intentions, we shall meet at Warsaw, I hope, and I shall reclaim a reward from your fair lips." Duroc then took his seat beside the Emperor, and the carriage drove rapidly off, while Napoleon waved a parting salute to the young woman.

The person who had made such an effort to see the Emperor, and welcome him to Polish soil, was Marie Walewska, *née* Laczinska. She was the offspring of a very old but poor and numerous family. M. Laczinski died when Marie was a baby, leaving six children, and the widow, who was absorbed in making the best of the small domain which constituted their fortune, sent her daughters to boarding-school, where they learned to dance, acquired a smattering of French and German, and a slight knowledge of music. Between fifteen and sixteen years of age Marie returned home, with but a mediocre education, but with a pure heart, which knew but two passions—religion and country—her love for her God was balanced by her love for Poland; those were the pivots upon which her nature turned, and to arouse her from her usually gentle sweetness it sufficed to say that she would marry a Russian or a Prussian, her country's enemies, a Protestant or schismatic. She had hardly returned to her home, when, by a singular chance, she had two excellent opportunities for marriage, and Mme. Laczinski permitted her daughter to choose between the aspirants for her hand. One was a charming young man who seemed to have everything in his favor, and who had pleased her from the first; he was very rich, well-born and remarkably handsome—but he was a Russian, and a son of one of those generals who had cruelly oppressed Poland. Marie could not consent to become *his* wife, so her choice fell upon the other suitor, old Anastase Colonna de Walewice-Walewska, who was seventy years of age, a widower for the second time, and whose oldest grandchild was nine years her senior, but he was very rich, the *Seigneur* of the province which the Laczinskas inhabited, owned most of the land, laid down the laws, inhabited *the château* of the neighborhood, and was the only person who invited his poor neighbors to dinner. He had been the late king's chamberlain, and on important occasions decorated his coat with the order of the White Eagle; he was the head of one of the most illustrious families of Poland, who were authentically connected with the Colonnas of Rome and bore the same coat-of-arms, and he was of more ancient lineage than any other family in the kingdom. It was not strange that Mme. Laczinska was enchanted at the prospect of having so illustrious a son-in-law, and Marie made little resistance, for her first appeal to her mother was met with an unanswerable argument; she fell ill, however, of an inflammatory fever, and for four months hovered between life and death. When barely convalescent she was led to the altar, and the miserable young woman spent three years in the dreary château of Walewice, finding her only consolation in her religion. At last she gave birth to a son and a desire for life re-awoke in her. She determined to live for her child, who had a right to the happiness which she had missed, but she did not wish that he should live upon annexed land which was no longer a country, that he should be, like her, in servitude, or that, like his father, he should beg of the conqueror his property and title; she wished her son to be a free man and a Pole, and to attain that end it was necessary that his country should rise and free herself.

Napoleon had already vanquished Austria, measured his strength against Russia at Austerlitz, and was about to strike at Prussia and her allies; he was a providential adversary of her country's enemies and seemed destined to save Poland.

When the campaign of 1806 opened and Napoleon's forces marched with incredible rapidity across France and Germany to Berlin, the Prussians melting like phantoms before them, Mme. Walewska reached such a state of feverish enthusiasm that she could no longer remain at Walewice, to which remote spot news penetrated but slowly, and her husband being as great a patriot as herself, they went to Warsaw, where they established themselves as became their rank.

Mme. Walewska, conscious of her lack of education and worldly knowledge, fearing to blunder when she spoke French, unsupported by family or friends, dreaded to go into society, and above all to appear at La Blacha, the palace of Prince Joseph Poniatowski, and the rallying-place of Warsaw's best society, and though in obedience to her husband's command, she made a few formal and obligatory visits, she held aloof from the gaieties of the capital, thus remaining, despite her loveliness, almost unknown.

The whole city was in a tumult of excitement over the approaching arrival of the Emperor, all being desirous that his reception at Warsaw should outdo the welcome given him at Posen; the city was turned topsy-turvy by the citizens in their determination to give Napoleon a royal welcome, for they felt that the fate of Poland lay in his hands. Mme. Walewska longed to be the first to greet him, and, without weighing the importance of the step she was taking, persuaded one of her cousins to accompany her and rushed to Bronie.

After the meeting which we described in the

beginning of the chapter she stood gazing after the imperial carriage until it was lost to view; then, carefully enveloping the bouquet which the Emperor had given her, she stepped into her carriage and returned to Warsaw.

Her intention was to keep her journey a secret, to shun all the fêtes and thus avoid a presentation to Napoleon; but her companion, though sworn to secrecy, was far too elated over the adventure to keep the story to herself, and one morning Prince Joseph Poniatowski sent to inquire at what hour Mme. Walewska could receive him, and, calling in the afternoon, invited her to a ball he was about to give in honor of the Emperor, saying that Napoleon wished particularly to meet her a second time. As she blushingly refused to understand his reference to her first meeting with His Majesty, the prince, laughing heartily over the matter, explained his knowledge of the affair. It appeared that at one of the dinners given in the Emperor's honor, he had been observed to look attentively at the Princess Lubomirska, and she was immediately presented, but after meeting her, Napoleon paid but scant attention to the lady; this indifference surprised Prince Joseph, but was explained by Duroc, who related the episode of Bronie, and explained that his royal master had fancied that in the princess he had discovered the charming unknown. Duroc gave all the details of the meeting at Bronie, describing minutely the face, figure and toilet of the mysterious lady, but Poniatowski was unable to divine who it could have been, and was about to give up his search in despair, when the indiscreet chatter of Mme. Walewska's companion enlightened him, and, knowing the Emperor's desire to cultivate the acquaintance, he determined that she should come to the ball.

Mme. Walewska refused absolutely to go, and remained unmoved even by his argument that under Heaven she might perhaps be an instrument towards the rehabilitation of her country. Hardly had the prince departed when the principal representatives of Poland were announced; they were statesmen, whose authority was based upon public esteem and consideration and the deference due to their irreproachable conduct and wisdom; all of these men foresaw what benefit might accrue to Poland from Napoleon's admiration for one of its daughters and they joined in urging her acceptance of the prince's invitation; their arguments, however, failed to move her and she was still firm in her determination to remain at home, when her husband arrived and came to their rescue. M. Walewska was ignorant of the adventure at Bronie, and saw in the insistence of these gentlemen nothing save the consideration due his rank and the services he had rendered his country, and promptly accepted for his wife. Marie pleaded, almost with tears, to remain at home, but her husband insisted, ridiculed her fears, and finally commanded that she should go. She made one condition, however, which was, that, as almost all the other ladies had already been presented, care should be taken that her presentation should not be conspicuous.

The great day came, and her husband hurried her toilet, fearing that they would be late and reach the ball-room after the Emperor had departed. M. Walewski would have liked to see his wife magnificently apparelled, and he found great fault with the severely simple dress of white satin which she had selected to wear and with the garland of leaves which was her only ornament; others, however, were not of his opinion, for a murmur of admiration greeted her entrance into the ball-room. She was installed between two ladies, with whom she was, unacquainted and was feeling strange and uncomfortable, when Prince Poniatowski stationed himself behind her. "Your arrival has been impatiently awaited, madame," he murmured, "and your entrance to the ball-room greeted with pleasure; your name has been repeated until it must be known by heart, and after scrutinizing your husband someone said, shrugging his shoulders: 'Poor little victim;' and I am commanded to invite you to dance."

"I do not dance," she answered, "and have no inclination towards that form of amusement."

The prince explained that his invitation, being at the instigation of the Emperor, was paramount to an order, that His Majesty was watching them and that if she refused he should be considered at fault, and also that the success of the ball largely depended upon her; but persuasion and explanation were alike wasted. Mme. Walewska positively refused to dance, and the prince had but one resource: to find Duroc, who received his confidences and repeated them to Napoleon.

Mme. Walewska was soon the centre of a brilliant circle of staff-officers who were charmed by her beauty and unaffected manners, for her presence, which was an open secret to the Poles, was not understood by the French. Napoleon, however, was not long in effecting the removal of his unconscious rivals; Louis de Périgord seemed the most devoted of her admirers, so the Emperor made a sign to Berthier and ordered him to send the aide-de-camp at once to the sixth corps on the Passarge, and the next in order was Bertrand, who, on a second sign, was ordered to report to Prince Jérôme before Breslau.

The Emperor wandered about the ball-room with the intention of making himself generally agreeable, but his preoccupation led him to make singularly *mal à propos* speeches ; he asked a young girl how many children she had, a homely old maid, if her husband was jealous of her beauty, and inquired of a lady who was enormously stout if she was very fond of dancing. When he arrived before Mme. Walewska her neighbors nudged her as a sign that she should rise, and standing, her eyes fixed on the ground, strangely pale, she awaited the Emperor's pleasure. "White upon white is not becoming, madame," he said aloud, then added in a low tone, "This is scarcely the reception I expected——" He paused and looked at her attentively, but as she made no response he passed on, and a few moments afterwards left the ball-room.

His departure was the signal for greater liberty of action, each recounting to her neighbor what the Emperor had said to her, and all anxious to learn what he said to Mme. Walewska, and to what he referred when saying that he had expected a different greeting, for those nearest had caught his remarks, and the wildest curiosity prevailed regarding it, some daring spirits even going so far as to question

Marie herself. As soon as possible she made her escape, but on the way home her husband also catechised her, and, receiving unsatisfactory replies, announced that he had accepted an invitation for a dinner at which the Emperor was to be present, and requested her to order a more elegant costume for that occasion. Marie was on the point of telling him of her imprudent trip to Bronie, of its consequences up to date and her disquietude; but he left her brusquely at the door of her room, which she had hardly entered, before her maid handed her a note which she had some difficulty in deciphering :

"I HAVE SEEN, ADMIRED AND DESIRED BUT YOU THIS EVENING. A KIND AND PROMPT ANSWER ALONE CAN CALM THE IMPATIENT ARDOR OF
"N."

Mme. Walewska crushed the note in her hand, disgusted and revolted by its language. "There is no answer?" she said to her maid, who departed to convey her mistress's reply to the bearer of the note; but the messenger who waited in the street was no other than Prince Poniatowski, who did not propose to be so easily beaten, and, despite the servant's remonstrances, entered the house and followed her to her mistress's room with such promptitude, that Mme. Walewska had barely time to lock the door. From behind the closed door she informed the prince that her decision was immutable; and at the risk of a scandal the prince alternately implored and menaced, but was at last obliged to depart, discomfited and angry. She was scarcely awake on the following morning, when her maid handed her a second note, which she did not open, but sealing it up in an envelope with the first ordered that both should be handed to the messenger.

Before noon her drawing-room was crowded, all the personages of the nation, influential members of the government, Prince Joseph and Grand Marshal Duroc, being assembled there, but Marie, pretexting a sick headache, remained in her own room stretched out upon a lounge. Her husband was furious, and to prove that he was not jealous, as was artfully insinuated, he conducted the prince and his countrymen into his wife's apartment, and in their presence insisted that she should allow herself to be presented and should attend the dinner, to which she was bidden. To this the Poles agreed in chorus, and one of their number, an old man, who was highly respected, and whose advice was deferentially listened to by the chiefs of the government, fixed his eyes sharply upon her, and said in an impressive manner: "I hope that between this and the date set for the dinner your indisposition will have disappeared, for you cannot refuse the invitation without laying yourself open to the accusation of lack of love for your country."

How could this inexperienced girl of eighteen, alone, without a friend to counsel her, defend herself against so many?—she did her best, but the pressure was too great. She was obliged to rise, and, obeying her husband's mandate, called upon Mme. de Vauban, who was Prince Joseph's mistress, solicited her advice as to the toilet she should wear, and asked her to be initiated into the mysteries of court etiquette; thus she was delivered into the hands of the enemy, for Mme. Vauban was deep in the intrigue.

Née Pugot-Barbentane, Mme. de Vauban had lived at Versailles and was familiar with the life of the old court; at the outbreak of the revolution she fled to Warsaw, and there lived publicly with the prince, who had previously been her lover. She thought that to give a mistress to a sovereign, whether he be Louis XV. or Napoleon, was the most important mission which a courtesan could fill, and as for scruples, purity, duty, or conjugal fidelity—it never occurred to her that a woman of the world would balance such virtues against certain advantages. Mme. de Vauban was clever enough to perceive that the woman with whom she had now to deal could not be tempted by worldly considerations, that she must manœuvre skilfully and make use of weapons with which she was not familiar, before she could overcome Mme. Walewska's scruples, and, feeling unequal to the task, she contented herself with paying her visitor numerous compliments, advising as to her dress and conduct, and protesting friendship; then she turned Marie over to a young woman who lived with her somewhat as a companion. This lady, Mme. Abramowicz, was a divorcée without fortune, young, gay, and clever, and, being nearer Mme. Walewska's age, possessed every requisite to attract her confidence, even the most exalted sentiments of patriotism— real or feigned. She insinuated herself into Mme. Walewska's confidence and won the affections of the lonely girl, who had never had an intimate friend, and whose heart longed for a confidante. Mme. Abramowicz ingratiated herself with the husband, and was inseparable from the wife, and when she thought that the time was ripe, she read to Mme. Walewska a letter, signed by the most prominent men of the nation, and members of the provisional government:

"MADAME:

"Slight causes sometimes produce great results,

and women from time immemorial have exercised great influence over the world's politics; ancient history, as well as modern, bears testimony to this fact, and so long as men are dominated by passion women can sway them.

"Had you been a man, you would gladly have given your life to your country; as a woman you cannot serve as her defender, but there are other sacrifices which you can make for Poland, and which you should gladly impose upon yourself, however painful they may be.

"Do you imagine that it was for love that Esther gave herself to Ahasverus? Does not the fact that he inspired her with such fear, that she swooned when he looked upon her, prove that affection had no part in that union? She sacrificed herself for her country, and, to her everlasting honor, she saved it. May history record as much for your glory and our happiness!

"Are you not daughter, sister, wife and mother to zealous Poles who, with us, form the national sheaf, the strength of which can be augmented only by the number and union of those who compose it. Remember, madame, the words of a celebrated man, a saint and pious ecclesiastic, Fénelon, who wrote: 'Men, in whom all public authority is vested, can achieve no effective result from their deliberations, if women do not aid in the execution of their designs.' Heed his voice, which unites with ours, that you may promote the happiness of your countrymen, of twenty million souls."

Thus every spring was brought into play to precipitate the downfall of this young woman, who, inexperienced and guileless, had neither a husband in whom she could confide, nor parents to defend her, nor friends anxious to save her ; the family, country and religion were invoked to force her compliance, all conspired against her, and to complete the work, she was made to read the note from Napoleon, which she had once refused to open.

"I fear, madame," he wrote, "that I have displeased you ; yet I had a right to hope the contrary —was I so mistaken ? Your enthusiasm has waned while mine has augmented. You have banished sleep from my pillow ! Ah, deign to give a little joy to a poor heart which is ready to adore you. Do you then find it so difficult to write to me ? You owe me two letters.

"N."

Her husband, proud of the success of his wife, for which he took all the credit, without understanding the situation nor having the slightest suspicion of what was expected of her—for he was an honest gentleman—insisted upon her going to the much discussed dinner. The poor girl herself understood that the step was a decisive one and committed her; but all the world wished it, and she yielded. Her drawing-room was constantly filled with visitors, who mutely felicitated her, and in order that she should not change her mind during the time preceding the dinner, Mme. Abramowicz kept her company.

On her way to the dinner, Mme. Walewska comforted herself with the idea that as she did not love Napoleon, she had nothing to fear, and on her arrival the marked attentions of some of the guests, who already had in view the solicitation of her protection, completely disgusted her with her supposed conquest and she was firmly resolved to remain unapproachable when the Emperor appeared. Napoleon was more self-possessed that evening than at the ball, and better prepared to be generally courteous; when Marie was presented he said simply: "I thought madame was indisposed, has she quite recovered?" and this purposely simple speech overthrew her suspicions and even struck her as being extremely delicate.

At table she was placed next the grand marshal

and almost opposite the Emperor, who, when all were seated, began in his curt fashion to question his neighbors upon the history of Poland; he appeared to listen attentively and to take a deep interest in the subject, but whether speaking or listening his eyes never left Mme. Walewska save to exchange a glance with Duroc, with whom he seemed to have established a sort of optical telegraph. It seemed as though the remarks which Duroc addressed to his neighbor were dictated by a glance or gesture of the Emperor, who kept up all the time a grave discussion upon European politics; once he lifted his hand to the left side of his coat, Duroc hesitated for a moment, looked attentively at his master, and at last, divining what was required of him, heaved an "Ah!" of satisfaction. It was the bouquet of Bronie which was in question and Duroc hastened to ask Mme. Walewska what had become of it.

Marie responded that she religiously preserved the flowers which the Emperor had given her for her son. "Ah! madame," said the grand marshal, "you must permit us to offer you something more worthy of you." Imagining that his speech had a double meaning she retorted loudly, flushed with anger: "I care only for flowers!" Duroc was dumfounded, but after a moment recovered his presence of mind sufficiently to say : "Very well, madame, we will pluck laurels from your native soil for you ; " and observing that that touched her, knew that his second speech had been a lucky one.

When the company rose from the table and returned to the drawing-room, the Emperor took advantage of the confusion to approach her and fixing upon her his strangely piercing eyes, the power of which no human being had ever resisted, he took her hand and pressing it, said in a low tone : "With eyes so sweet and tender, with such an expression of goodness, it cannot possibly be a pleasure to torture a man, or else appearances are deceitful and you are the most coquettish of women, the most cruel of your sex."

On the Emperor's departure the party broke up and Mme. Walewska was persuaded to go to Mme. de Vauban's where a number of the dinner guests and those who were initiated into the intrigue, awaited her coming ; upon entering the room she was immediately surrounded by those who flattered her and assured her that the Emperor had had eyes only for her, that she alone could plead the nation's cause, touch his heart and determine him to rehabilitate Poland. Little by little, as if in obedience to some secret understanding, the guests departed, leaving Marie and Mme. Abramowicz alone; almost immediately Duroc was announced and when the doors were closed, he seated himself at Mme. Walewska's side and laid a letter on her knee, then taking her hand, said in the gentlest possible manner: "Can you refuse the request of one who has never brooked refusal? His position, though glorious, is lonely and sad, and it lies in your power to give him some hours, at least, of happiness." Duroc spoke at great length but she made no answer and hiding her face in her hands wept and sobbed like a child; the other woman, however, answered for her and guaranteed that she would go to the rendezvous. When Marie indignantly remonstrated, she shamed her with her lack of patriotism, telling her, that she was a renegade daughter of Poland, that they should all willingly sacrifice anything for him who would be their country's deliverer, and finally bowed the grand marshal out, assuring him that Mme. Walewska would finally comply with his master's wishes; then opening the note which he had brought, Mme. Abramowicz read it aloud:

"There are moments when the weight of my rank seems more than I can bear, and I am now living through such a period. How can I satisfy the desires and needs of a hungry heart which longs to throw itself at your feet and is arrested only by weighty considerations which paralyze its most ardent desires and deprive me of freedom of action? Oh, if you would but come to me! You alone can surmount the obstacles which separate us; my friend Doroc will arrange everything.

"Come to me, and all your desires shall be fulfilled, and your country will be dearer to me when you have taught me to love it.

"N."

Thus the fate of Poland lay in her little hands; it was not her countrymen alone who said so, but the great conqueror himself, who affirmed it; it depended upon her, that her country should be reborn, the shameful divisions abolished, the torn parts reunited, and the White Eagle fly proudly over all. It was no wonder that such a glorious dream almost intoxicated her; yet she still struggled, claiming that she was not equal to playing such a rôle, to which they answered, that she should not lack for advisers, and had only to follow their counsel. Her modesty revolting, she was told that the sentiments she entertained were provincial, ridiculous and out of date, that many another woman, quite as virtuous as she, would willingly exchange places with her and lend Poland the aid of their beauty were the chance given them,—why, they asked, should she doubt her ability to do good? Though an Emperor,

Napoleon was but a man—and a man in love; she would be able to wind him around her finger and achieve the realization of the patriot's brightest dreams. Thus at last they wrung from her a reluctant consent. She refused, however, to answer Napoleon's letter, feeling physically incapable of writing, and they left her alone to advise together, taking the precaution, however, to lock her in, lest she might change her mind and run away; but she was not thinking of such a thing, she reflected, or rather, exhausted by the prolonged struggle, she dreamed.

She wondered if she could not without losing her self-esteem have an interview with Napoleon, inspire him with friendship and respect and persuade him to listen to the prayer of her people; surely he would not force his caresses upon her, knowing that she had no love to give him, for she would tell him that he inspired her only with sentiments of enthusiasm, admiration and gratitude. There was nothing depraved in the imagination of this girl of eighteen, whose only knowledge of love was derived from the almost platonic affection of her septuagenarian husband, and drifting into the world of dreams, where the virtue of woman has nothing to fear from the passions of man, where the senses are abolished and souls speak and understand each other, she dreamed of an ideal friendship, which should both comfort Napoleon in his loneliness and benefit Poland.

The conspirators, having settled everything, returned and Mme. Walewska agreed to comply with all their wishes, only stipulating that she should remain where she was until those who were to conduct her to Napoleon, should call; she remained all the next day, which dragged by slowly, alternately watching the hands of the clock and the closed door by which her executioner must enter.

At half-past ten in the evening some one knocked, and Mme. Abramowicz, hastily arraying Marie in a hat with a thick veil and a long cloak, which completely disguised her figure, led her like one in a dream to a carriage which waited at the street corner, and assisted her to enter it; a man with a long coat and a slouched hat, who had held the door open, drew up the step and took a seat beside her. Not a word was exchanged on the way, and when the carriage drew up before a private entrance to the grand palace, her silent companion assisted her to leave the carriage and almost carried her to a door which was opened impatiently from within, and, quietly departing, left her alone with Napoleon.

Blinded by tears Mme. Walewska could not discern the features of the Emperor who knelt by her side, took her hand, and began speaking to her in a caressing manner; nor was she clearly conscious of what he said until the words: "Your old husband" escaped him, when the full realization of the ignominy burst upon her and with a cry of horror she sprang to her feet and looked about for means to escape.

Napoleon was momentarily paralyzed with surprise, not knowing what to make of this woman, who after so many entreaties had yielded to his solicitations and granted him a nocturnal rendezvous, yet who now manifested such unmistakable and unaffected horror at her situation. Not holding the key to her presence there, he questioned an instant if she was not acting a part with the intent to increase his desire, but her grief and dismay were too genuine, and determined to solve the riddle of her conduct, he drew her gently away from the door against which she was leaning, seated her in an arm-chair and began to question her kindly regarding her history; resolved not to alarm her, he sought to put his questions in a manner which would least wound and shock her sensibilities, but in spite of his kind intentions, his habitual masterfulness pierced the veil of gentleness and he could only obtain brief and fragmentary answers from the trembling woman, but even those he turned to weapons against herself. "Had she voluntarily given herself to the man whose name she bore, was it for rank and wealth that she had sacrificed her youth? No;—then who forced her to unite her young life with an old and decrepid man? Her mother;—then why had she any remorse, since the marriage was not of her chosing?" Marie stammered between her sobs that it was her duty to be faithful, that that which God had joined together, man should not seek to sunder. Napoleon could not control his mirth, and at the sound of his laughter Mme. Walewska's tears fell all the faster.

More and more mystified and correspondingly interested by this woman, the like of whom he had never before encountered, he was the more determined to discover the solution to her presence in his apartments. Here was a woman who wished to be a faithful wife, to hold fast to the principles of her religion, a woman who was unquestionably pure and virtuous, and yet, she was there in his apartments at the dead of night, in compliance with his wishes. Never had his curiosity been so aroused, and he pressed his questions, asking about the education she had received, the life she had led in the country and the society she frequented, of her mother and family,—he wished to know everything, even to the name she had received at baptism : the sweet name of Marie, by which he ever afterwards called her.

At two in the morning some one rapped at the door. "What!" exclaimed Napoleon, "so soon? Well, my gentle dove, dry your tears and go home to rest; you need never again fear the Eagle, for he will exert no other influence over you than that of passionate love. You will end by loving him, for he will be everything to you—everything." He assisted her to fasten her mantle, put on her veil, and conducted her to the door, but before he let her out he exacted a promise that she would return the following night. She was reconducted to her home and retired almost reassured, it seemed as if her dream might be realized, for as Napoleon had been kind and tender and spared her that time, she fancied it would be the same in the future.

At nine o'clock the following morning the confidential friend was at her bedside, holding in her hands a large package, which, after prudently locking the door, she carefully unwrapped, and drew forth several jewel-cases in red morocco, a quantity of hothouse flowers intermingled with branches of laurel and a sealed letter; but scarcely had she exposed to view a magnificent brooch and spray of diamonds than Mme. Walewska snatched them from her hands and flung them to the end of the room, furious that they should have been sent her. She ordered that they should be immediately returned;

she wished the Emperor to comprehend that she was not for sale, and that if she gave herself to him it would not be from a desire for jewels; then, unsealing the letter, she read:

"Marie, my sweet Marie, my first thought is for you, my greatest desire to see you again; you will keep your promise and return, will you not? Otherwise the Eagle will fly to you! Our friend tells me we shall meet at dinner, deign, therefore, to accept this bouquet which shall establish between us a bond by which we may communicate in the midst of the crowd which will surround us, and even under the gaze of others. When I lay my hand over my heart you will know that it is filled with thoughts of you and you can respond by touching your bouquet. Love me, my precious Marie, and never take your hand off your flowers.

"N."

The letter was all very fine, but it could not make her accept his diamonds, nor even the flowers and laurels. She had an excuse ready: One did not wear flowers on one's dress save at balls, and it was to a dinner she was going. She vainly essayed to excuse herself from this dinner, but she was forced to fulfill her engagement by those whose ambitions were roused and who firmly believed that, through her, they would see their dearest wish fulfilled. Her husband remained perfectly blind, he never suspected for a moment the intrigue which was being carried on about him, and urgently desired her to accept all invitations.

On her arrival at the house where the dinner was given, she was immediately surrounded by her acquaintances and by those who were anxious to be presented, and it seemed to the poor woman as if all these strangers were cognizant of her adventure of the night previous. The Emperor had already arrived and appeared dissatisfied, he frowned and regarded her with an angry expression, his eyes seeming to read her very soul; as he advanced towards her she trembled, fearing that he was going to make a public scene, when suddenly recalling the words of his letter, she laid her hand on the place where his flowers should have been, and had the satisfaction of seeing his contracted features relax into a smile and his hand respond by a similar sign. Before going to table he called Duroc aside and spoke with him for an instant; she had barely taken her place at the table, where, as at the preceding dinner, she was seated next the grand marshal, when he attacked her about the bouquet; she responded haughtily that she was insulted by the diamonds, and wished it distinctly understood that she would accept no presents of that kind, that the only thing which could repay her devotion was hope for the future of her country. "Has the Emperor not already given you the right to hope?" retorted Duroc; then he recalled to her a number of acts which proved his master's good faith, and throughout the dinner he continued to talk of the Emperor's affection for her, the loneliness of his high state, and the need he had of a heart which would love and understand him, and of the glory of the mission which was hers, reminding her, too, of her promise to return to the palace that night.

She was conducted to the palace with the same precautions as on the previous evening, and found Napoleon gloomy and thoughtful. "You have come at last," he said, "I had abandoned all hope of seeing you!" He assisted her to lay aside her cloak and hat, and when she was seated, stationed himself before her, and commanded her to explain her conduct. Why did she go to Bronie? Why had she sought to inspire him with a sentiment which she did not share? Why had she refused his flowers and even the laurels? Why had she ever made a rendezvous with him? What were her intentions when she came to the palace? As she did not answer he gave way to a paroxysm of anger and exclaimed:

"You led me to hope for everything and you give nothing; you are a true Pole, and your actions confirm the opinion I have always held of your nation."

Moved and troubled by her reception, and anxious to know what he thought of her people, she said: "Ah, Sire, forgive me, and tell me what you think of us Poles."

He informed her that he considered the Polish race passionate and unstable, emotional and lacking in system; that their enthusiasm was impetuous and genuine, but short-lived, and that this portrait of her race was her likeness. Had she not flown, like one crazed with enthusiasm, to gain a glimpse of him? Had she not led him to believe by her earnest and passionate expressions of esteem that she was most kindly disposed towards him? He had allowed himself to be duped, but she must know that, when anything was withheld from him, it became the object he most coveted, and that nothing could daunt him in the pursuit of it. Whether real or feigned, the violence of his excitement grew apace and Mme. Walewska shrank before him. "I want you to understand," he thundered, "that I will force you to love me! I have already lifted the name of your country from the dust, thanks to me that it has not been wiped from the face of the earth! I will do more—but, remember, that even as I crush this watch in my hand, so shall your country and all your hopes be crushed if you push me to extremes, repulse my love and refuse me yours."

Overcome by this violence, Mme. Walewska fainted—when she recovered consciousness she no longer belonged to herself.

Henceforth it was a *liaison*, if one can so designate the habit she acquired of going nightly to the palace and passively submitting to caresses which she hoped would some day bring her a great reward. Napoleon established a provisional government, the embryo of an army and several companies of light cavalry were attached to his guard; but it was not for so little that Mme. Walewska had sacrificed her virtue, the only thing which could content her and condone her conduct in her own eyes, was the re-establishment of Poland as a nation and a state. Incapable of feigning a sentiment which she did not entertain, or a passion which she did not feel, she had none of the requisites for the domination of a lover, and was not even cunning enough to conceal the motive which actuated her. Nightly she referred to the one topic which interested her and was consoled by promises and buoyed by hopes; but the promises were always for the future, in the present there was only misery which seemed interminable.

She met with no censure in her own country;

aside from her husband, whom she had been obliged to leave, all hastened to do her honor, not as a favorite but as a victim, for none were in ignorance of her sacrifice, and by all she was esteemed, respected and pitied. Her husband's own sisters, Princess Jablonowska and Countess Birginska, constituted themselves her chaperones; had she so desired, she could have taken the first place in Warsaw's society and maintained almost regal state; but Mme. Walewska shunned society, lived unpretentiously, and gave no cause for enmity; therefore, though less flattered, she received greater sympathy.

To a society which concealed oriental habits under a veneer of French elegance and customs, which still retained the moral code of Catherine the Great, there was nothing shocking in Mme. Walewska's position. There was no fine Polish gentleman of the time who had not an authenticated mistress, of whose existence his wife was well aware and to whom she exhibited no animosity; scarcely a noble did not support, at some one of his country seats, one or more Georgian favorites; consequently, as he did not travel with a harem in his train, Napoleon appeared to the Poles as a singularly chaste sovereign; when he established himself in Warsaw they felt that he should have a female companion to divert him, and but natural and right to secure for him the society of the only woman in whom he manifested the least interest.

Fortuitously, the Emperor admired a woman of exceptional character and one who could be made politically useful; virtuous, unaffected, disinterested, animated solely by love of country, incarnating in her person the best traits of her nation, Marie Walewska was capable of inspiring in the heart of her royal lover a deep and lasting affection, and the Poles reasoned that she would become like a second wife to Napoleon, that, without sharing his imperial state and splendor, she would fill a special place in his life and be an ever-present ambassadress for Poland.

Napoleon was alive to the fact that Mme. Walewska did not love him for himself, that her country held the first place in her heart, indeed, she never essayed to make him think otherwise, but frankly avowed that she had become his mistress in the hope of softening his heart and awakening his sympathies towards her unhappy land, and he, who usually mistrusted any one whom he suspected of a desire to make use of him, placed implicit confidence in this simple, sincere and earnest girl; he knew her to be so far above the ordinary ambitions of women that he longed to content her, and keenly regretted his inability to bestow the one boon she coveted.

"Rest assured," he frequently said to her, "that my promises to you shall be fulfilled. I have already forced Russia to relinquish what she had usurped; time will do the rest, but you must be patient; politics is a cord which snaps if subjected to too great a strain, and the time is not yet ripe for the realization of your hopes. In the meanwhile, your politicians must work, the country must be organized; you are rich in patriots and can command plenty of brave arms—honor and courage start from every pore of you Poles—but that will not suffice, there must be great unanimity."

It was strange how this man, who never discussed politics with a woman, continually recurred to the subject of Poland's future, and discussed with her the best means for the amelioration of her countrymen, how to benefit all classes and insure a united movement even if at the expense of the aristocracy.

"You well know," he said, "that I love your nation, that my wishes and my political views lead me to desire its entire rehabilitation; I am most willing to second its efforts and uphold its rights, and all that I can do without endangering the interests of France, I will do; but remember that the distance that separates us is tremendous, that what

I establish here to-day may be annihilated to-morrow. My first duty is to France, I cannot shed French blood for a cause which is not theirs, nor arm my people and rush to your succor each time that it may be necessary."

From these grave matters he would turn to social gossip, current anecdotes and the tittle-tattle of the drawing-room with a rapidity which amazed his listener. He wanted her to inform him regarding the private life of every personage whom he encountered, his curiosity was insatiable and went into the minutest details ; it was his way of forming an opinion upon the leading class wherever he found himself, and here, where such great interests were at stake, he made use of every means to inform himself. From the accumulated tales, which engraved themselves upon his memory, bits of information regarding this one and that one, he drew astute conclusions which astonished the woman who listened and showed her that she had furnished him with arms against herself ; she would protest indignantly against the deductions he drew and the judgments he pronounced ; the quarrel usually ending with his giving her a slight tap on the cheek and exclaiming : "Good little Marie, you are worthy to be a Spartan and to have a country !"

Napoleon would not have loved Mme. Walewska

as he did, had he not taken an interest in her toilet, in which matter he considered himself an excellent judge, having once written to Savary: "You know that I am an authority upon woman's dress." From the time of the Consulate he had selected the presents sent to any queen, and the dress of the court ladies did not escape his criticism; even Josephine, whose taste in dress was exquisite, was not exempt. Above all he disliked sombre costumes, and Mme. Walewska insisted upon dressing in the most simple fashion and always in black, white or gray, which displeased him extremely, and regarding which he remonstrated with her, and she retorted, that "a Polish woman should wear mourning for her country; when you resuscitate it I will wear nothing but rose-color."

Thus in every way she brought him back to the same subject, but without annoying him, so great was his love for her. It did not suffice him to see his mistress by appointment, he desired that she should attend all the dinners and fêtes at which he was obliged to be present, and as he wished to be constantly in communication with her he initiated her into the mysterious system by which he communicated with Duroc, and she became more expert at it than the grand marshal himself, and at the very instant when Napoleon seemed engrossed in some serious subject he would tell her in his sign language that his heart was filled with thoughts of her. When she expressed her astonishment that so great a general, so shrewd a politician, should condescend to such boyish means of communication, he said: "Reflect that I am obliged to fill with dignity the post assigned to me, I have the honor to command nations. I was an acorn, I have become an oak and I am watched on every side; this situation obliges me to play a rôle which is not always easy, but which I am obliged to keep up in order to preserve the character with which I am invested, and while I must play the monarch for all the world, I love to be your subject, and how can I manage to tell you that I love you at a state dinner (which I want to do every time I look at you), unless I employ the sign language?"

When he removed his headquarters to Finckenstein Marie was obliged to follow him, and the melancholy existence she led there resembled closely that which she had once led at Walewice with her old husband. The long, quiet days were broken only by the meals which she ate *tête-à-tête* with the Emperor, and which were served by a single valet, the rest of the time was spent in reading and embroidering, and her only distraction was watching the parade from behind closed blinds. It was the life of a recluse subject to the will of a master, without society, pleasure or distraction, and yet it satisfied her better than the brilliant society which she had left at Warsaw. Thus Mme. Walewska realized the type of woman which he had hoped to find in Josephine : sweet, complaisant, timid, attentive, unambitious and seemingly without will, who lived only for him and who, though she asked a favor of him, asked so colossal a one that it became impersonal and impossible of conception save by a soul singularly pure and disinterested, and to hope to receive it from the hands of a mortal, was to think of him almost as a god ; all this appealed strongly to Napoleon and augmented his Polish love's hold on him.

When the Emperor was about to leave Poland, without having realized the dream for whose sake Mme. Walewska had given herself to him when, despairing and disillusioned, Marie refused to follow him to Paris and announced her intention to retire into the heart of the country, there to await in sadness and solitude the fulfilment of his vows, it became his turn to supplicate : "I know," he said, "that you can live without me, that your heart is not mine ; but you are good, kind and generous, can you find it in your heart to deprive me of my only happiness—of the few moments that I spend each day with you? You are my sole joy, the one being who brightens my life, and yet I am supposed to be the most highly blessed of mortals." His tone was so bitter, his smile so sad, that, overwhelmed by a new sentiment of pity for this master of the world, she promised to follow him to Paris.

Mme. Walewska reached Paris in the beginning of the year 1808, and thenceforth this mysterious *liaison*, to which Napoleon was sometimes unfaithful, but which was nevertheless the grand passion of his life, was established on so strange a footing that, if one could not find its confirmation in isolated details and dates which are authenticated by divers witnesses, it would be difficult to follow the chain of events and one would not dare to affirm the continuity of facts which the best informed contemporaries ignored.

It is known that during the campaign of 1809 Mme. Walewska went to Vienna, where an elegant establishment awaited her near the Palace of Schœnbrunn, that she became *enceinte*, and after peace was declared went to Walewice for her confinement, and that there, on the 4th of May, 1810, Alexandre-Florian-Joseph Colonna-Walewska, was born. Knowing so much, have we not a right to question whether Napoleon's hesitation when treating with Austria, his indecision regarding the fate of Poland was not due to the presence of her to whom he had solemnly promised the rehabilitation of her country?

What contemporaries do not tell us is that towards the close of 1810, Mme. Walewska, accompanied by her sister-in-law the Princess Jablonowska, and her infant son, returned to Paris, where she lived first in a pretty house on the Chaussée d'Antin, afterwards at No. 2 rue du Houssaie and then at No. 48 rue de la Victoire. Every morning the Emperor sent to ask her orders; boxes in all the theatres were placed at her disposal; the doors of the museums opened to her; Corvisart was charged to look after her health and Duroc to see that her every desire was satisfied and her life made as agreeable and easy as possible. The following anecdote gives an example of her power:

At Spa, a young Englishman indulged in a joke of doubtful taste at the expense of the Princess Jablonowska. On her return to Paris the Princess invited him to accompany Mme. Walewska and herself to the museum of artillery; in the gallery where armor was displayed the party stopped before the armor worn by Jeanne d'Arc, and while the young man was looking at it the Maid of France opened her arms and, seizing him, pressed him violently to her heart; suffocating, he struggled to escape, but it was only upon the order of Mme. Walewska that Jeanne d'Arc released him. Knowing the jealousy with which Napoleon guarded his museums, is this not a positive proof of her power?

Whenever he could escape from the cares of state the Emperor went to her, or had her come to the château with her son, upon whom he had conferred the title of count of the Empire. None in the company, with the exception of the Poles, suspected their relations, and Mme. Walewska went little into society and received only a few compatriots; her household was mounted upon a modest footing and her conduct extremely circumspect. When she went to take the waters at Spa her sister-in-law accompanied her, and it was at her sister-in-law's home, a house at Mons-sur-Orge, called the château de Brétigny, which was rented from the Duchesse de Richelieu, that she passed the summer. They essayed vainly to draw her into society, but her greatest preoccupation was to hide from the world the relations of which the majority of women would have been proud. Her country home was situated in a secluded spot and conducted in an extremely simple style, but it was her universe, and she left it as seldom as possible; nevertheless, she was obliged to accept Josephine's repeated invitations to go to Malmaison with her son, whom the Empress loaded with presents and playthings, but it does not appear that she mingled in court society before the year 1813, and it is only at that epoch that in her personal accounts two court-dresses are mentioned; one was a dress of black velvet with gold-spangled tulle, the other of white tulle; however *recherché* her costumes may have appeared she was certainly not an extravagant woman, for her annual bills at Leroy's never exceeded six thousand francs.

It was needless for her to appear at court in order to recall herself to Napoleon's memory, proof of which lies in a letter written by him from Nogent, the 8th of February, 1814; in the midst of the terrible strain incident to the French campaign, on the day following the battle of Brienne, and on the eve of that of Champaubert, he thought of Mme. Walewska and endeavored to secure her future. He had charged the treasurer-general, M. de La Bouillerie to settle fifty thousand pounds upon the young Count Walewska in such fashion that, in the event of his death, his mother should be his heir, and the idea that all the formalities had not been fulfilled caused him to write this letter:

"I have received your letter relative to young Walewska, I give you *carte blanche* to do whatever is proper; but act at once. That which preoccupies me most at present is first that boy and then his mother.

"N."

Mme. Walewska knew nothing of all this, and there never was a more disinterested heart than hers. During the last days at Fontainebleau when the Emperor, abandoned by all, had sought to find in death a refuge which destiny refused him, she hastened to his side and spent an entire night in an antechamber awaiting his commands. Napoleon, absorbed in his gloomy reflections, exhausted by the physical crisis through which he had passed, never thought of asking for her until she had already been gone an hour. "Poor woman," he said, "she will believe herself forgotten."

He little understood her, for a few months later, at the end of August, 1814, she landed at Elba, accompanied by her son, her sister and her brother, Colonel Laczinski, and spent a day with the Emperor at the hermitage of Marciana. From the moment she learned of Napoleon's return to Paris in 1815 she was among the most devoted and assiduous of the women who visited the Elysée and at Malmaison, faithful to the Emperor through his fall and misfortunes.

But after he had gone to St. Helena she thought

herself free, and M. Walewska having died in 1814, she married at Liège in 1816, General Count d'Ornano, who had been obliged to take refuge there after the second return of the Bourbons. General d'Ornano had been one of the bravest officers of the Grand Army, and Mme. Walewska's union with him was brief but happy, for she died within the year, expiring in her home in the rue de la Victoire on the 15th of December, 1817.

One of the Emperor's companions at St. Helena tells us, that the news of Mme. Walewska's marriage affected His Majesty keenly, as he had preserved a warm affection for her and could not reconcile himself to the thought that one whom he had loved should care for another. In his will the Emperor had expressed his desire that Alexandre Walewska should enter the French army; his career was a brilliant one, and as soldier, writer, diplomat and statesman his life is too intimately associated with the history of his time to render it necessary for us to dwell upon it here.

CHAPTER XVI.

THE DIVORCE.

THE death of Napoleon-Charles destroyed Napoleon's dream of creating an heredity by adoption; the birth of Léon disabused his mind of all doubts of his inability to create a direct line, and love for Mme. Walewska completed the work by weakening Josephine's influence. It is impossible that at Tilsit the Emperor directly negotiated an alliance with a Russian grand-duchess, but certain that from the moment of his return to France he began paving the way for divorce; his ordinary method of procedure was to carry a project into operation as soon as it was conceived, but he took two years for the execution of this one.

Mentally Napoleon was fully alive to the advantages which would accrue to him from a divorce and second marriage, but, though his brain was willing, his heart's dictates were in opposition to his political sagacity, and it was this war within himself which kept him in a state of uncertainty from 1807 to 1809, an uncertainty which causes his actions to appear inexplicable to the historian, cannot be accounted for by political reasons, and was due solely to conscientious scruples.

Before Napoleon could acquire the energy necessary for the rupture of his marital relations with the woman whom he had once passionately loved, and raised to share the throne with him, who was bound to him by ten years of close companionship, and whom, with her children, he had preferred above his own flesh and blood, it was essential that the ties which bound him should break one by one, and a divorce became a necessity.

Feeling that he was about to do her a great wrong, Napoleon attributed to Josephine even more amiable qualities than she possessed, and repeatedly said to his advisers: "She will not be able to bear it, it will kill her!" and possibly he was superstitious enough to believe that his fortunes depended upon her and her star; yet neither vain superstition, fear of the criticism of his companions in arms nor of public opinion, caused his hesitation, he simply paused for a time, listening to the dictates of his heart.

Weary of the Emperor's vacillations some of those who were ardent advocates of the divorce, such as Fouché, essayed to hasten the rupture by adroit insinuations to Josephine, with the view of determining her to take the initiative and voluntarily sacrifice herself. Napoleon understood that this excess of zeal rose from the projects he had formed and allowed to be divined, but the more he realized his weakness the more it irritated him, and, indignant that one of his ministers should fancy he could coerce him, that this police spy should have dared to probe into his domestic life and show his ugly face in the conjugal chamber, he treated Fouché as he had never treated any man before, and Josephine, astutely advised by Talleyrand, who for some reason or another wished to throw an obstacle in Fouché's path, profited by her husband's momentary indignation and boldly accused him of intending to repudiate her, Napoleon shrinking from the scene which was bound to follow an admission of his intention, hesitated and was reconquered.

This renewal of affection for his wife did not render him more faithful, for in the sentiment which he entertained for Josephine, fidelity had no part; it was a kindly feeling, combined from memory, pity and gratitude, but permitting of no illusions regarding the youth and beauty of his wife, and when he found himself in the society of younger and prettier women he saw no reason why he should not enjoy it without detriment to his marital relations.

During the sojourn at Paris and Fontainebleau, between August and October of 1807, Mme. Gazzani exercised her influence over Napoleon, and it is said that at Fontainebleau he also fell a victim to the charms of Mme. de B. ****, who was a companion to the Princess Pauline. This Mme. de B. **** whose husband was distantly related to the Beauharnais and owed his place at court to his kinship with them, was one of the prettiest of women; she was very tall, and some claim that her head and features were too small for her figure, but she was generally considered a remarkably handsome woman; she was extremely clever, poor, and morally unprejudiced. The Emperor saw her at first at a hunting-breakfast and signified his admiration for her, going so far, it is said, as to write to her. Her apartment was on the first floor of the château, and gave into the garden of Diana, so it was conveniently situated for nocturnal visitors, and His Majesty was always welcome. Mme. de B. **** was well content with her position, and the husband, who was aged and little troubled by scruples, rubbed his hands over it. "My wife," he said one day, in a drawing-room, "is a woman of wonderful resources; we are not rich, yet, thanks to her cleverness, we appear to be; she is a perfect treasure." She worked so well that she made him a chamberlain to one of the Emperor's imperial brothers and a baron of the Empire. This *liaison*, however, was conducted with such secrecy that some have doubted if it really existed, and as it was not continued after the Emperor left Fontainebleau, the complaisant husband's pleasure abated and he had some unpleasant experiences, for Mme. de B. * * * * quarreling with the princess because of a brilliant young officer, was dismissed from the imperial household and obliged to retire to her country-seat, while the officer was sent to Spain, where he was grievously wounded; on his return, Mme. de B. * * * * secured a divorce and they were married.

Although Bonaparte had allowed Josephine to reassume her sway over him he was still haunted by the thought of divorce, the wisdom of which his counsellors never permitted him to forget, and it was with this step in view that he went to Italy in 1807. One of Josephine's greatest disquietudes in connection with the divorce was the effect it would have upon her son, for although Napoleon had established Eugène in Italy as viceroy in 1805, and had married him, in 1806, to the Princess Augusta, giving him the title of "Son of France," his promises had not been sanctioned by legislative act; he wished, therefore, to reassure both his wife and the House of Bavaria, and also to inform himself regarding a union which had been proposed to him, namely, a marriage with the Princess Charlotte of Bavaria, and it was doubtless with this alliance in view that he arranged a meeting at Milan with the Bavarian king, queen and princess. The young girl, however, proved less prepossessing than he had anticipated, and discarding the idea of that alliance he left the princess to her strange destiny, and considered the advisability of a family alliance.

Although Lucien Bonaparte's first wife, Catherine Boyer, was a woman of most humble origin, the uneducated daughter of an innkeeper at Saint-Maximin de Vâr, Napoleon had loved her like a sister, and her young daughter, Lolotte, having reached a marriageable age he seriously considered the advisability of making her his wife. There was an estrangement between his brother Lucien and himself, and the Emperor, who considered family unity essential, was desirous of effecting a reconciliation, and argued that this step might cement Lucien's affection for him; he reasoned that if the dissimilarity between Lolotte's age and his proved too great and the young girl showed any repugnance at the idea of becoming his wife, or if, on close acquaintance with her, he should alter his intentions, it would be easy to find her a suitable husband from some of the royal houses of Europe. He thought that, should the marriage take place, the succession which he would establish in France would be more purely Bonaparte, and hoped that the girl who had been very fond of him as a little child would find it easy to renew the affection of her youth. Lolotte was brought to Paris and placed under the protection of her grandmother, Madame Mère, but she did not remain long. She amused her father with her letters about the doings of the French court, seemingly unsuspicious that her correspondence was watched, and it was soon clear to Napoleon that a union with his niece was not feasible, whereupon he sent her back to Italy. Lolotte Bonaparte never wore a crown, but in 1815, she married the Prince Gabrielli, and lived until 1865.

The Italian journey, then, was unproductive as far as Napoleon's matrimonial projects were concerned, but Fouchè continued to agitate and disseminate the idea of divorce, thus exposing himself to wrathful letters from the Emperor, which did not, however, cause him to cease intriguing; his ordinarily clear perception seemed obscured, his usual sagacity at fault, for he failed to see that this was not the moment to urge his plans. The perils of Eylau, and the conspiracy which was hatched during his absence had not made sufficient impression upon the Emperor for him to deem it essential to leave a living representative in Paris when war called him away, and in order to decide him to repudiate Josephine and wed another an extraordinarily desirable alliance must be proposed : such a one was not at hand, the idea of a Russian alliance having long been abandoned, and Austria having no marriageable daughter to offer.

Almost immediately following Napoleon's return from Italy, Mme. Walewska arrived in Paris and Napoleon's heart was completely filled with her, while his mind was occupied with affairs of state ; the Spanish question perplexed him greatly, and claiming that that must be settled before he could reopen with Alexander the conference begun at Tilsit, he gave little thought to the question of divorce. Talleyrand, however, began to urge the step, and to insist that the Emperor should at least come to some decision upon the subject. Under the pressure brought to bear upon him Napoleon became so excited and nervous that a serious illness seemed inevitable ; he had frequent attacks of excruciating stomach trouble, and when ill would draw his wife down beside him on the bed and weeping sob out that he *could* not leave her.

It seemed as if Josephine possessed some talisman by which she held her husband's affection, and although he sometimes said that she was old and ugly, during their sojourn at Marrac his conduct towards her was like that of a youthful lover. In those days he apparently forgot that a divorce had ever been talked of; they amused themselves like a couple of children let loose from school; frequently, in the presence of the guard of light cavalry that escorted them, he chased Josephine across the beach and pushed her into the water, laughing like a boy, and when the Empress, in her haste, lost her shoes, he threw them out to sea and forced her to drive home in her stockings, that he might the better see and feel her feet, which he greatly admired. At this period he was more alive to Josephine's worth than ever before, indeed she never appeared to better advantage than upon this journey to Bayonne; she showed herself intelligent, adroit and full of tact in the strange interview they were obliged to hold with the Spanish sovereigns, and later during the triumphal march across the south and west provinces, when the temperature was so high that in order to be at all comfortable they were obliged to travel by night, when at each halting place they were fêted and entertained in exactly the same dull manner, when Napoleon was bored in the extreme by the ovations, Josephine, in spite of fatigue and illness, was always punctual and ready with a gracious smile and fitting word for all. It was wonderful how she managed to appear interested in everything, in household affairs and children, in all which could best please the women; how she managed to temper Napoleon's dominant power by her gracious smile and caressing manner and to win love where he won admiration. She had wonderful tact in giving a present, and a way of taking a jewel from her own person and offering it to a matron or maid which was simply captivating, and understood how to make the presentation to an official of an obligatory present appear like a token of personal esteem.

Although for four months constantly under the charm of Josephine's presence, the desire for divorce again took hold of Napoleon; doubtless it was the incentive for the journey of Erfurt, to which place he was accompanied by Talleyrand, whose mission it was to insinuate to the Emperor Alexander that Napoleon was ready to share his throne with one of the grand duchesses; but Talleyrand, instead of serving his royal master, unscrupulously betrayed him; it was he who furnished the Russian Emperor with a plan for eluding Napoleon's proposal, suggested the basis for a new coalition against France, and paved the way for the war of 1809.

From Erfurt, Napoleon was obliged to return at once to Paris and the Spanish frontier. He relied upon Alexander's good faith, and fancied that when he had quelled the Spanish mutiny, nothing would be easier to arrange than the proposed Russian alliance. However, it was not a mutiny which he had to subdue in Spain but an insurrection, and, instead of taking two months to put it down, as he had anticipated, he was detained three months, and finally achieved but a barren victory. Then came news from Paris of plots in his own family, who were figuring upon his death, that Austria was again in arms, that the archdukes were instigating revolt in Germany, and the sacred war kept alive by secret societies. Leaving Benavente, he spurred to Paris with incredible rapidity, and in three months he unmasked traitors, put his affairs in order, organized an army, and pushed on to the Danube, Austria having attacked and Archduke Charles invaded the territory of the confederation; but when at Schoenbrunn, after seventeen months of indefatigable action, he had time for reflection, the urgent necessity for divorce was made apparent; he not only realized clearly the obligation of assuring an heredity, but the necessity of having a representative in Paris during his absence, one around whom his friends would rally in the case of an English invasion or an uprising of the royalists.

Josephine was no longer at hand to confuse and

trouble him by appeals to his conscience, and the memory of the years they had passed together, to startle him by suggesting that, with the sundering of their lives, the star of his destiny would begin to wane; another woman, as agreeable, younger, and more beautiful, next whose heart lay a child of his, was at his side, and so the question, which for two long years had vexed his spirit and wrung his heart, was finally settled. So long as Napoleon doubted if he could have children he had schemed, planned and invented every imaginable combination for the foundation of an heredity, but now that he *knew* that he could found a line of kings, that his descendants might sit upon the throne of France, it was plain to him that a second marriage was the only practical step, that a direct heir alone could ensure the stability of the Empire.

In order to spare both Josephine and himself, and avoid further painful scenes, he wrote from Vienna ordering that the communicating doors between his apartments and the Empress's at Fontainebleau be walled up, and when Josephine joined him at the château, he refused to grant her a private interview and remained closeted with his ministers; from that time, he so arranged that they were never alone together, and thus avoided any explanations or private conversation regarding his intentions. Napoleon essayed to make Hortense announce his decision to her mother, and, when she refused, summoned Eugène from Italy for the purpose ; but when he knew his stepson to be on the way, he mustered up his courage and provoked the supreme conversation wherein he must declare to his wife his irrevocable determination to divorce her.

So at last fell the blow which Josephine had been dreading for years, for the avoidance of which she had deployed all her charms, the fear of which had poisoned her life ; she knew that further effort was futile, and although she wept and fainted when the Emperor finally announced his decision, it was rather with the view of making the best of the situation for herself and children than from excess of feeling ; she wished her son's position firmly established, her own debts paid, and an ample income settled upon her ; she desired to preserve the rank and prerogatives of an Empress, and above all that she should not be forced to leave Paris. Napoleon granted all that she asked, the Elysée was given her as a town residence, the domain of Malmaison for a country seat, and the château of Navarre as a hunting-lodge ; and a yearly income of three millions, the title, the escort, and the customary retinue of a reigning Empress were assured her ; thus he prepared for his divorced wife a place in the state which was unparalleled in history, unless a like example could be found among the annals of Rome and Byzantium.

But Napoleon gave his divorced wife more than money, palaces and titles, he gave her his sympathy and his tears. He sent almost hourly for news of her, desiring to know how she passed her time away from him, and like the most faithful and tender of lovers, wrote her letter after letter, and insisted that all who surrounded her should visit him that he might glean from them every item of interest regarding the daily life of the woman he had repudiated; there was no attention, kindness, or favor that he did not lavish upon her, so conscious was he of the wrong he had done; what he wished was that she should accept the inevitable with fortitude, and, making the best of her new situation, relieve him of the pain of knowing her unhappy through his will.

Nevertheless, when he went to Malmaison to see and console Josephine he never embraced her or entered her private apartments, but so arranged that his visits should have an air of formality, for he wished that both she and the world should know that all was ended. This conduct bears witness to his respect for Josephine, showing that he would not permit any one to think that the wife of yesterday had become the mistress of to-day; perhaps, too, he doubted of his ability to maintain his distant demeanor save when supported by witnesses, and his conduct shows how strong, powerful and tender was his affection for this woman; an affection which had outlived youth and beauty, and, in spite of all strains, remained to the last the great love of his life.

CHAPTER XVII.

MARIE-LOUISE.

Up to this period all the women with whom Napoleon had been intimately connected had been considered by him as his inferiors, for, surrounded by women of the noblest blood of France, Montmorencies, Mortemarts and Lavals, he had learned to estimate the social worth of the Beauharnais family correctly, and the influence which Josephine had exercised over him through her supposed prestige had long since vanished. None of his mistresses had been sufficiently high-born to flatter his vanity by her rank and worldly position; indeed, he does not seem to have attempted conquests of that kind, or, if he did, must have been early discouraged; moreover, in order to satisfy his egotism and ambition something more than a marriage with a noble family of France was necessary. Such an alliance was made possible by the Emperor of Austria's proffer of the hand of his eldest daughter Marie-Louise; this alliance Napoleon believed would assist him to

MARIE LOUISE.

climb the last step towards equality with his predecessors upon the French throne, and the Napoleonic system which he had endeavored to establish and to strengthen by intermarriages between the Bonapartes and the various reigning families of Europe, would, by his marriage, become amalgamated with the house of Austria, even as the Bourbons had been before him, his dynasty would lose its improvised air, and on assuming the quartering of the house of Austria gain the relationships which seemed to him to constitute the only strong and durable political tie.

In this alliance Napoleon's ambition found satisfaction, but how could his dominant spirit accommodate itself to a wife who had from birth the consciousness of her rank and worth, and the belief in her own infallibility common to those born in the purple. By a strange hazard the young girl who was offered to him had been so educated as to have no will save that of her father, to realize that her interests were subordinate to those of her nation, that she was destined to play a rôle in some political combination, and that she must accept without a murmur the marriage which the political interests of her country imposed upon her; it was with this object in view that Marie-Louise's character had been moulded from earliest infancy. She had been taught all languages, German, English, French, Italian, Spanish, Turkish, Bohemian and even Latin, for it was impossible to foresee where her destiny would lead her; moreover, it was argued, that the more extended her vocabulary, the greater the number of words at her command for the expression of an idea, the less ideas she was likely to have. Her talents for music and drawing had been encouraged and cultivated as those accomplishments provided an innocent means of distraction for a princess wherever she might find herself; the teachings of the Church had been given her literally, and minute attention to all its forms inculcated, but all questions of dogma were avoided, for it was possible that fate would give the Austrian princess a heretic for a husband. Her education included a system of morals which only the casuists of Spain could have advised; the archduchess was kept in ignorance regarding the difference in sex, the barnyard was peopled only by hens, she had no little dogs, only bitches, her riding horse was a mare, her books were pitilessly expurged, pages, lines, even words being cut out, without its occurring to the censor that the gulfs thus created would give the archduchess food for thought. The princess was continually under the surveillance of a court lady, who directed the management of her apartments, was present at her lessons, invented her games, and watched the servants and teachers; this lady never left her pupil, either by night or day, and, as politics played an important part in the princess's destiny, the incumbent of this position changed with each new ministry, and Marie-Louise had five governesses in eighteen years; her education, however, was regulated by such rigid laws that, despite all changes in her suite, she remained the same.

Marie-Louise's amusements were such as are common to a conventual life; she had flowers to cultivate, birds to take care of, and sometimes lunched under the trees with her governess's daughter; her holidays were spent in the intimacy of the family in pleasant but *bourgeois* fashion; she never participated in the gaieties of the court, and had made but one or two short journeys in order that she might have change of air. The event which had made the greatest impression upon her, and which had given her the most distraction, were her flights before the French invasions, when discipline had been relaxed and tasks laid aside; thus it was not a woman who was offered to Napoleon but a child, accustomed to live under such strict rules that any life would seem sweet by comparison, and for whom the simplest pleasures would possess a charm.

Marie-Louise's education was identical with that

given to the daughters of Marie-Thérèse and the result of this method, as exemplified by Marie-Antoinette at Versailles, Marie-Caroline at Naples and Marie-Amélie at Parma, was not desirable—and it was to be dreaded lest the nature of the young Austrian princess which had been so repressed would expand in the same way as her aunt's; Napoleon, however, reasoned that husbands are responsible for their wives' conduct, and laid his plans accordingly. The school-girl who was to pass into his keeping should simply leave the convents of Schoenbrunn and Laxenburg for that of the Tuileries and Saint-Cloud, she should live under the same inflexible rules, the same rigorous surveillance, she should have no freedom in the choice of friendships and read no book which had not been previously scanned; no masculine visitors should be permitted, and her governess should be replaced by a lady of honor and four ladies-in-waiting who should be perpetually on guard; the only difference in her life should be the presence of a husband.

Thus since the husband was obliged to teach his wife all that her parents had taken pains to conceal from her, he resolved to supplement the enlightenment by great precautions, and determined that no man, however high or low his position upon the social ladder, should remain for one instant alone with the Empress. He re-established the etiquette of Louis XIV.'s time, the rigidity of which had been relaxed through the indifference of Louis XV. and the feebleness of Louis XVI. ; but where royalty veiled its distrust under the disguise of traditional honors, employing the highest ladies in the land to watch the queen under the pretext of keeping her company, Napoleon brought into play undisguised military discipline ; he was not actuated by jealousy, but simply by motives of prudence and precaution ; he had once said at a state's council : "Adultery is the affair of a moment," and he was convinced, perhaps by experience, that a *tête-à-tête* between a man and a woman easily became criminal. With such a distrust of woman Napoleon would doubtless have found the Oriental system quite to his taste, but as it was not customary among Europeans to seclude their wives in a harem he was obliged to replace eunuchs by ladies-in-waiting, and iron bars by etiquette, but, save for the name, the prison was the same. The imprisonment accepted, he intended to give to his wife every material pleasure which she could desire ; but the pleasures which he offered her were almost identical with those which a Sultan gives to his favorite odalisque.

While at Vienna Marie-Louise ignored the pleasure of elegant dresses, exquisite laces, rare shawls and dainty linen; in Paris, provided that no merchant approached her and she made her selections through the medium of a lady of the wardrobe, she should have every beautiful thing which French industry could produce, and Napoleon gave her a foretaste of the luxuries which were to be hers in the *corbeille* which he sent her, of which he inspected each article and had it packed under his supervision. The *corbeille* included twelve dozen chemise of the finest batiste, trimmed with embroidery and valenciennes, twenty-four dozen handkerchiefs, twenty-four night-dresses, thirty-six skirts, and twenty-four night-caps, at a cost of fifty-one thousand, one hundred and fifty-six francs.

In addition the *corbeille* contained eighty-one thousand, one hundred and ninety-nine francs' worth of laces, exclusive of a point-d'Alençon shawl, which was valued at three thousand two hundred francs; sixty-four dresses from Leroy costing one hundred and twenty-six thousand, nine hundred and seventy-six francs; seventeen cashmere shawls valued at thirty-nine thousand, eight hundred and sixty francs; twelve dozen stockings, ranging in price from eighteen to seventy-two francs a pair, and sixty pairs of shoes and slippers of all colors and fabrics, which had been made according to measures sent from Vienna, and were so small that Napoleon, as he examined them, remarked that it was a good sign. Everything that Paris could produce that was beautiful and rare was presented to her, and yearly she might have almost as much. As for her toilet alone, she was to have an allowance of thirty thousand francs a month.

As a girl, Marie-Louise had owned but one or two jewels, whose value was so insignificant that the wife of a Paris shopkeeper would have disdained them; a couple of hair bracelets, a necklace of seed pearls and another of green beads had comprised her ornaments; as Empress she was to have diamonds of enormous value; the thirteen stones which surrounded the portrait which the Emperor sent her alone cost six hundred thousand francs, a diamond necklace costing nine hundred thousand francs, and a pair of ear-rings costing four hundred thousand francs, and a still finer parure composed of a diadem, comb, ear-rings, necklace and belt contained two thousand, two hundred and fifty-seven large stones and three hundred and six rose diamonds. She was to have a parure of emeralds and diamonds valued at two hundred and eighty-nine thousand, eight hundred and sixty-five francs; one of opal and diamonds costing two hundred and seventy-five thousand, nine hundred and fifty-three francs; one of ruby and diamonds and another of turquoise and diamonds, all of immense value, without counting the diamond ornaments furnished by the crown and appraised at three million, three hundred and twenty-five thousand, seven hundred and twenty-four francs.

The apartments which she had inhabited in Austria had been furnished in the simplest manner, in France magnificent rooms which had been re-decorated and furnished under the Emperor's personal supervision awaited her coming, and in order to spare her any feeling of strangeness the Emperor ordered that all toilet articles and small pieces of furniture likely to be in daily use should be duplicated; thus, in whatever palace she went to reside, the articles to which she was accustomed should be at hand. When the work of the furnishing of the apartments was complete the Emperor was so proud of his success as a decorator that he invited all his guests to view them, and at the Tuileries he himself conducted the king and queen of Bavaria to inspect the rooms, taking them by the way of a dark and narrow staircase which led from his own dressing-room to the Empress's bed-chamber; the staircase was so narrow that the king, who was extremely corpulent, was obliged to descend sideways, and when they arrived at the foot, the door leading into the apartment destined for the Empress was found to be locked and they were obliged to turn about in the dark and narrow space and remount the staircase—a movement which was executed with great difficulty because of his Bavarian Majesty's great size. At Compiègne it was the Emperor also who did the honors of the Empress's bathroom to the Queen of Westphalia, displaying to her the marble bath and furniture and hangings of India stuffs which had cost four hundred thousand francs.

For the good of her stomach Marie-Louise's governesses had forbidden all rich food, but the Emperor, foreseeing that, like most Viennese, she would have a taste for goodies, took upon himself the ordering of her table, multiplying the deserts with cakes and ices and bon-bons.

Marie-Louise had a generous nature, but up to the time of her marriage had had nothing to give save such samples of her own handicraft as she had been taught to make; as Empress she was enabled to shower presents upon her family, Napoleon setting her an example by sending handsome presents to her people even before she arrived in France. It was not possible to assert that she had a taste for the theatre, as she had never seen a play, but Napoleon believed that she would not be of her country and her time if she had not, and planned for her amusement in that way, both when she accompanied him to the theatre or preferred to have the actors play in the palace ; in short it was his intention that she should have everything which would distract and amuse her so long as it was in accordance with the secluded life he had planned. It was not his intention that she should leave her apartments save for great civil and religious ceremonies, state balls, the theatre, the hunt, and such journeys as might be necessary, and upon these occasions she was to be surrounded by her ladies of honor and officers, and, arrayed in court costume, laden with jewels, she was to remain in haughty isolation, to be worshipped by all classes from afar like an idol.

Thus he essayed to gild the bars of the prison which he had prepared for the Austrian princess, dreaming to keep her a child, and imagining that she would pass, without feeling the transition, from captive archduchess to captive empress ; thus he sought to assure himself of her fidelity and so to arrange her life that she should be, like Cæsar's wife, above suspicion. The woman whom he thus planned to seclude had in his eyes a mission to fulfil, to be the mother of his children ; she was the mould destined to receive and develop the dynastic germ, and it was in order to assure the legitimacy of his descendants that he took so many precautions : he acted not unwisely, for the doctrine of monarchical succession hinges upon the unquestionable legitimacy of offspring.

Napoleon did not doubt that Marie-Louise-would become a mother, having informed himself minutely regarding her health and physical being, and knowing her family to be prolific, her mother having had thirteen children, her grandmother seventeen, and her great grandmother twenty-six, and he was impatient for her arrival that he might insure the future of his race.

Napoleon had received Marie-Louise's portrait, which represented a young woman with long, blonde hair parted in heavy masses and brushed back on each side from a high forehead, eyes of china blue, a nose slightly indented at the base, thick lips, heavy chin, white but rather prominent teeth and a complexion marred by the ravages of smallpox; the shoulders were large and white, the bust remarkably full, and the arms, which were long and thin, terminated in small and pretty hands, while her foot was charming. He had been told that she was tall for a woman, and neither graceful nor supple, but an easy carriage Napoleon thought could be acquired, and what he most desired was that her appearance should show the characteristics of her race.

When Lejeune, General Berthier's aide-de-camp,

arrived at Compiègne, preceding Marie-Louise by several days, Napoleon had the portrait which he had received from Vienna brought into the room and proceeded to question the young officer as to the likeness; happily Lejeune was an artist as well as a soldier, and was able to show the Emperor a sketch in profile which he had himself made of the archduchess. "Ah," exclaimed Napoleon, "she has the real Austrian lip!" and going to the table upon which lay a number of medals with the heads of various Austrian sovereigns thereon, he compared the various profiles and recognized with pleasure that his future Empress was a true Habsburg.

From the moment the negotiations were concluded, that he knew his dream about to be fulfilled, Napoleon burned with impatience for possession; in vain he essayed to distract his thoughts by hunting, but the idea haunted him; he spoke of it to every one and he wished the preparations for the reception finished before they had begun. On its being represented to him that it would be difficult to turn the *grand salon* of the Louvre into a chapel because of the immense pictures which it was difficult to dispose of, he responded: "Well, then, burn them!"

He was preoccupied with the impression which he would make and he ordered from Léger, who was

Murat's tailor, a court costume literally covered with embroidery, but on trying it on found it so uncomfortable that he was unable to wear it. He ordered boots from a new shoemaker, in order to have finer shoes than those he had hitherto worn and took dancing-lessons, wishing to learn to waltz, but he only succeeded in bringing on an attack of heart trouble, which forced him to abandon the lessons. As Catherine of Westphalia wrote to her father: "Neither you nor I would ever have imagined Napoleon capable of such things."

In measure as the cortège from Vienna advanced his impatience increased. At last he could wait no longer. Marie-Louise slept at Vitry on the 26th of March, on the 27th she was due at Soisson, and it was not until the 28th that the Emperor was to join her. The programme of the ceremonial was printed, the pavilion where the meeting was to take place was built and decorated, the troops were commanded and the repast prepared, nevertheless, on the morning of the 27th, in a pouring rain, Napoleon left Compiègne in company with Murat, and without an escort or suite, rode to Courcelles where he awaited Marie-Louise's coming under the shelter of a church porch. At last the coach with its eight horses appeared and stopped for relays, Napoleon advanced to the side of the carriage, the groom of the chambers announced him, his sister Caroline, who was conducting the bride, presented him to Marie-Louise, and dripping with rain he entered the carriage, which drove rapidly off. They rushed past villages where the mayors, address in hand, waited to receive them, through cities *en fête* and at last, at nine o'clock in the evening, without having broken the day's fast, they arrived at Compiègne. The Emperor cut short the addresses of welcome, presentations and compliments, and, taking Marie-Louise by the hand, conducted her to his private apartment; there the young girl had reason to remember the lesson which her father had instilled—obedience to her husband in all things.

The following noon the Emperor had his breakfast served at the Empress's bedside by one of her maids, and during the day he said to one of his generals: "My friend, marry a German, they are the best women in the world, good, amiable, innocent, and fresh as a rose." Napoleon appears to have disregarded or disdained the criticisms which would naturally follow upon his action in assuming that the marriage by proxy was all that was necessary, and his consummation of it before the subsequent ceremonials had taken place, and justified his conduct by saying: "Henry IV. did the same."

MARIE-LOUISE.

PART II.

THREE months after her marriage Marie-Louise said to Metternich: "I am not afraid of Napoleon, but I begin to think he is of me." Thus three months had sufficed to banish the terrible fear which from Vienna to Compiègne had caused her such mortal terror that it had affected her physical well-being. But how was it possible that Napoleon should have become timid in the presence of this girl of eighteen? In taking this Austrian princess to wife he realized the dream of years, and from a purely physical desire for the possession of the high-born girl had grown a desire to be the object of her affection, as well as the husband assigned her by the political interests of her country; he wished to know that he possessed her heart, and desired that she should proclaim her happiness.

One morning when they were at the Tuileries the Emperor sent for Metternich and closeted him with the Empress; at the end of an hour he rejoined them and said to the ambassador: "Well, have you had a good talk, has the Empress laughed or cried, had she many complaints to make?" Then, seeing that the ambassador was embarrassed, he added: "Oh, I do not expect you to give me a detailed account of your conversation; it is private matter between you and the Empress;" nevertheless, on the following day, he questioned Metternich minutely, and as the latter was not inclined to enlighten him, he exclaimed: "The Empress has no complaints to make, and I hope you will say so to your sovereign, as he will rely implicitly upon what you say." In reality it was rather himself than the Austrian emperor whom he sought to reassure; he wished to believe that his wife was devoted to him, that she was contented with the life he forced her to lead, and hid from him no lingering sentiment of distrust and dislike. Aspiring to domestic peace and happiness, he longed for the assurance of Marie-Louise's affection and the realization of his desires.

From childhood the Austrian princess had shared the universal hatred of Bonaparte. When only six years old her mother had told her that Monseigneur Bonaparte, the Corsican, had fled from Egypt, deserting his army, and had become a Turk; she believed firmly that he had been in the habit of beating his ministers, and had slain two of his generals with his own hand, and the year preceding her marriage—the year which had seen Vienna bombarded, and witnessed the battles of Eckmühl, Essling and Wagram—she had considered him one of the most despicable of beings. After Znaïm Marie-Louise wrote to a friend: "I am consumed with fury against Napoleon, yet I am obliged to sit at table with one of his marshals;" and when his divorce was announced, and the question of a second marriage began to be discussed she never admitted for a moment that the French conqueror's choice might fall upon her. "My father," she said, "is too kind to coerce me in a matter of such importance." She pitied Napoleon's possible choice, being sure that it would not be she who would be the victim of political expediency; and when the project of her marriage was discussed, she wrote to a friend of her childhood: "Pray for me, for, while I am ready to sacrifice my personal happiness for the welfare of my country, I am most unhappy." Though in reality the Austrian princesses had no voice in the disposal of their hands and no opinion save that of their father, for form's sake, Marie-Louise's consent to the marriage was asked, and she resigned herself to the inevitable, while mentally regarding her future husband as an ogre. When one considers the situation her feeling was not unnatural; four times the French conqueror had devastated her country, twice he had entered Vienna as a victor; he had forced her royal father to go to his camp, suing for peace; every sentiment of patriotism and filial affection, the most sacred of human emotions, the most sensitive chord in noble pride had been outraged by him; yet, strange as it may appear, Marie-Louise once wed her repugnance was not apparent. Whether this was due to the education which she had received, or whether her natural temperament was awakened and she enjoyed the good things which Napoleon provided for her—luxuries to which she was unaccustomed,—and found his personality not displeasing, or whether her contentment was feigned, it is impossible to affirm; but it is probable that the first supposition is correct, and Napoleon did all in his power to prove to her that he was, and would remain, a good husband. At the beginning of the Consulate he had ceased to share his chamber with Josephine, pretending that his work and duties rendered it necessary, but in reality, to insure his own freedom; he was prepared, however, if Marie-Louise exacted it, to reassume the chain, for he said: "It is a woman's rightful appanage;" but their temperaments were too dissimilar; while he, always chilly, wished a fire kept up all the year round, she, accustomed to a cold climate and a

Spartan-like existence in the immense and glacial palaces of the environs of Vienna, could not stand heated rooms. Frequently, with the uxoriousness of a young husband, he urged Marie-Louise to spend the night with him, but she always responded that he kept his rooms too warm ; while on going to her apartments he would find the temperature too low for him and order a fire lighted, but he invariably deferred to Marie-Louise's contrary opinion with the remark that "Her Majesty's will was law," and, after shivering for a short period, would go away.

This difference in their temperaments and indifference on her part paved the way for infidelities, but Napoleon does not appear to have thought of such a thing, or, if he did, he hid his *amours* carefully and they were but passing. In 1811 he appears to have paid some attention to the Princess Aldobrandini-Borghèse, *née* Mlle. de Rochefaucauld, to whom he had given a dowry of eight hundred thousand francs and married to the brother-in-law of Pauline Bonaparte, and whom he had just named lady-in-waiting ; but it is probable that he simply admired the manner and elegance of the young woman, who is said to have been charming. There was also some talk, and some gossip in private correspondence, regarding the Duchess of Montebello, who was one of the Empress's ladies of honor, but there is no proof of a *liaison;* such adventures as he did permit himself were obscure and carefully dissimulated, creating no gossip, simply because no one knew anything about them. The first *amour* which caused any gossip had its birth at Caen where the Emperor met Mme. Pellapra of the Testa-Cubières suit. Napoleon again met Mme. Pellapra at Lyons on his return from Elba in 1815, and then pamphleteers attacked "Mme. Ventreplat" to their hearts' content. At Saint-Cloud there was a little love-affair with a certain Lise B **** but it never reached serious proportions; beyond this his marital behavior towards Marie-Louise was exemplary.

Bonaparte imagined that the young Empress felt aggrieved at his visits to Josephine at Malmaison and to Mme. Walewska in the rue de la Victoire, although the former had become yearly less frequent in proportion as Josephine's conduct became more and more displeasing, and were made with great privacy, while the latter were so secret that few were cognizant of them. On the officers who composed his suite when he visited Malmaison and on those who were aware of his friendship with Mme. Walewska he imposed caution and secrecy, saying on each occasion: "Knowledge of this visit would cause my wife unnecessary pain." After his second marriage his entire manner of life changed; there remained to him from his poor, solitary and melancholy youth, which was devoid of the amusements natural to his age, a taste for noisy and active sports and in that respect he, with his forty-one years and Marie-Louise with her eighteen, were well matched; if possible he was the bigger child of the two, and he entered with zest into amusements suitable for a collegian. The young Empress had proposed but one amendment to the cloister-like existence mapped out for her, she desired to ride horseback, which was an exercise habitual with the princesses of Lorraine as soon as they escaped the maternal rule; Marie-Antoinette had done the same, and there is a record of Marie-Thérèse's objurgations. Napoleon himself acted as riding-master to his young wife, and during the first lessons ran at her horse's side, bridle in hand, until she had acquired sufficient confidence to ride alone, then daily the horses were ordered immediately after breakfast, and, without taking time to put on his boots, the Emperor would throw himself into the saddle, and in his stocking-feet gallop up and down the Grande Allée after his wife, exciting the horses to run and greatly amused by her cries and laughter; about every ten feet a groom was stationed in order to avoid any accident to the Empress, but it often happened that the Emperor had the most falls. In the evening, in the intimacy of the household, he organized all kinds of games, such as blind-man's-buff, puss-in-the-corner, cushion-and-keys and games of forfeits in which he took an active part. Up to this time Marie-Louise's only social accomplishment was the ability to move her ear without moving a muscle of her face, but she now learned to play billiards, for which game she developed such a passion and so much talent, that the Emperor was obliged to take lessons of one of his chamberlains before he could meet her on equal terms; she also had a fancy for sketching his profile and he was always ready to pose for her, although he refused to sit for any painter; he listened attentively, when, seated at the piano, she played German sonatas, although he had but little taste for that style of music, and manifested a proper degree of interest when she showed him the suspenders or sash she was embroidering for him. He was always at her side, devoted and attentive, endeavoring to amuse and distract his " good Marie-Louise," and his *bourgeois* habit of addressing her in the second person amazed the court, which had returned to the rigid etiquette of Louis XIV.'s time. Such an existence and such manners did not shock Marie-Louise, she soon accustomed herself to the new manner of life and addressed her husband with the familiar "thou," gave friendly nicknames to her sisters-in-law and called Madame Mère "mamma"; but all this affability rested upon a condition, that her husband should never leave her, but should always be at her disposition, and he who, up to that moment, had regulated his days according to his occupations and the demands of state, was now constrained to conciliate his occupations—sometimes to sacrifice them —to the tastes and caprices of his wife.

It had previously been the Emperor's habit to breakfast alone and hurriedly, upon the corner of his writing-table (when business permitted him to breakfast at all), but he resigned himself to breakfasting with his wife at a fixed hour, taking from affairs of state the time for an elaborate repast which was most distasteful to him. Between the years of 1810 and 1812 the royal pair took five long journeys, visiting Normandy, Belgium, Holland, the Rhine and Dresden, and it was not she who waited for the Emperor as Josephine had done, it was the husband's turn to cultivate his patience, for Marie-Louise was never on time for any social function; he made all his personal tastes subservient to hers and was not only a faithful but a loving and attentive husband, never missing an occasion to give his wife a pleasure. The magnificent present which he made his wife of a *parure* of Brazilian rubies, costing four hundred thousand francs, when she had only wished for one valued at forty-six thousand, and the superb necklace, consisting of eight strings of pearls, which cost five hundred thousand francs, which he presented to her after her confinement and which was stolen from Blois, were simply imperial. The fact which shows the lover in the husband were the manifold little presents which he gave her, such as bracelets, bearing the date of some occasion which had been particularly joyous, loving words or names spelt out in precious stones, and was it not a proclamation of her affection when she had her own portrait framed in precious stones whose initial letters formed the words "*Louise, je t'aime,*" and placed it upon her husband's writing desk.

If Napoleon had not loved his young wife he would not have taken umbrage at the slightest reference to his affection in the newspaper or to a verse wherein he was represented as a love-sick shepherd; as it was, the moment he saw the slightest reference to his affection in print he felt as though its sanctity had been violated, and immediately wrote a furious letter to the minister of police, wherein he did not deny his love, but insisted that the newspapers should not be permitted to comment upon it. Thinking to strengthen his wife's affection, he showered valuable presents of every description upon each member of her family, and favors upon all the Austrians at his court.

Despite time, the love which Marie-Louise manifested, and the precautions for his marital security which he had taken, and which were still carefully observed, he continued to be suspicious, and when the war with Russia called him from home he arranged that a detailed account of his wife's daily life and actions should be sent him by each courier; these letters were written by an illiterate person upon the commonest of paper, and upon these wretched scrawls he, who was usually so scrupulous and critical, wrote questions and notes; and yet in spite of this continual surveillance he dared not openly take his wife to task when anything displeased him, but strove to find an intermediary to express his disapproval.

Upon one occasion the Empress, while walking in the park at Saint-Cloud with Mme. de Montebello, allowed the duchess to present one of her relations and spoke with him for some moments; the following morning after the levee the Emperor detained the Austrian ambassador and recounted the affair, and upon Metternich's feigning not to comprehend what was wanted of him, Napoleon frankly explained that he wished the ambassador to speak to the Empress, and the Austrian refusing he insisted, saying:

"The Empress is young and might misunderstand my motives, attributing them to jealousy, while what you would say to her would make quite a different impression."

Napoleon's best beloved mistress, she who had most occupied his thoughts, was power, and this power which he had refused to give to Josephine, of which he had been so jealous that neither his two oldest counsellors, his brothers, nor any living being had he ever even given a shadow of authority, he gave, in 1813, in that time which was most perilous for his empire, to Marie-Louise ; making her regent of the Empire.

Doubtless there was more shadow than substance in this abandonment, and that no grave decision could be taken without his consent; it is probable that a premonition of disaster assailed him even in Russia, and that by this act he intended to assure the transmission of his crown, but in any case it entailed a stripping of some of his dearly loved authority, and he had not hesitated. Decrees were signed in his name by the Empress, by her pardons were accorded, nominations made and proclamations issued ; the bulletins by which, since 1800, the master announced his victories, distributed his glory and gave the accounts of his conquests, were things of the past, and it was : "Her Imperial Majesty,

Queen and Regent, who had received from the army information," and the conscripts for the unfortunate army were called "Marie-Louise men" by the people.

From head to foot of the governmental ladder weaknesses manifested themselves and treachery succeeded. Napoleon was no longer there, even his name had disappeared, while that of Marie-Louise was feared by none and meant nothing to the people; still, Napoleon would not alter his decree, applauded the step he had taken, and believed that his wife knew more than Cambacérès or than all the Bonapartes put together, and the nearer the catastrophe, the more imminent the peril, the more tenaciously he clung to the idea that she, she alone, would be his salvation.

By chance—for she was not responsible for his departure from Paris, the capitulation and all the rest—Marie-Louise caused his final downfall. Napoleon wrote her a letter, not in cipher, wherein he indicated the movements which he intended to attempt against the allied armies; this letter fell into the hands of Bluecher's courier, and General Bluecher made haste to lay it, *with the seal broken*, at the feet of the august daughter of his Imperial Majesty the Emperor of Austria

CHAPTER XVIII.

ELBA.

It is doubtful if Napoleon was actuated solely by love in the pursuance of the course described in the preceding chapter, and highly probable that his actions were entirely due to motives of policy. He probably argued that when the Austrian Emperor found himself face to face with his daughter and grandson as the representatives of France, he would hesitate to strike the blow which would ruin them, and that the sovereigns of Europe, not finding himself, but one of their own rank seated upon the French throne, would hesitate to overthrow it, and, believing themselves interested in the tranquillity of France, would accept and confirm the substitution, that though he himself might be forced to abdicate, the dynasty which he had established would be assured.

In order to admit the truth of this hypothesis one must admit that, from the year 1813, before Lützen, before the first campaign, wherein he constantly manifested his confidence in his continued success, Napoleon was at heart despairing; that he had latent doubts about Austria, and considered Marie-Louise as a pledge of coalition, trusted in the bond of paternity, and relied upon the good faith of Francis II., the father.

To divine such a conspiracy as the aristocrats of Europe had woven against him, to foresee that the young girl who had been given him as wife was the lure prepared by the allied oligarchies to entrap him, would have required an insight into the depths of royal unscrupulousness which even a Talleyrand and a Fouché might be incapable of.

In order to conceive and carry out such a design, to coalesce around a nuptial bed the hate of all the old dynasties, the profound corruption which is met with solely in the highest circles was alone capable; in these circles education and tradition have rendered men unscrupulous, they become accustomed to disregard all laws, human or divine, which militate against their interests and to carry their designs into execution regardless of the means employed, seeing therein no dishonor. In this instance it was not a mistress but a wife which had to be furnished to encompass their object, and what mattered it if the wheels of their triumphant chariot, while crushing the impious being who had outraged the sacred monarchical system, also rolled over the shuddering form and blonde locks of an archduchess. Should she survive the ordeal, means should be found to console her, should she die—well, it could not be helped, for the attainment of such an end something must be risked and Marie-Louise was only a woman.

Napoleon never suspected such a despicable conspiracy, never admitted that his wife was the accomplice of his enemies; nor was she, for care had been taken to conceal from her the rôle she was destined to play, and she enacted it the better because of her innocence. It was not until much later, at Saint Helena, that Napoleon traced the continuity between his second marriage and the disasters which followed it; even then he did not sound the plot to its very depth, either because it displeased him to elucidate the principal reason of his downfall, or because it pained him to smirch the memory of his wife by connecting her with so vile a scheme. He frequently remarked: "My marriage was a flower-covered pit which they dug for me;" and instead of harboring resentment against this woman who had been the cause of his downfall, he showed her more affection and greater confidence, as if to console her for the pain and disillusion caused by the aggressiveness of her native land and the menacing attitude of her father, which he believed she could not fail to regard as treacherous towards her and hers.

When the campaign of 1812 opened Napoleon apparently entertained no doubts of his ultimate success, it was his nature to hope even against hope, and it was not until much later that he was forced to admit the possibility of the enemies entering Paris and carrying away the Empress and the King of Rome. He believed that theirs would be but a brief triumph, for the momentary occupation of Paris did not alter his strategic plans, but he could not suffer the thought that his wife and son should be, even momentarily, hostages in the hands of his adversaries, and it was to spare them such an insult that he ordered Joseph to abandon Paris, thus taking from it its statesmen and resisting elements and compromising the entire edifice of his plans, for Talleyrand knew how to avoid the injunction to follow the court. His plans had long been laid, he had ingratiated himself into the confidence of King Joseph, the Empress, the prefecture of the Seine and the police; he had accomplices everywhere over whom he exercised a strong and inexplicable influence and who seemed bound to him by an infernal pact; and with them he accomplished, in 1814, the treason which he began to plot at Tilsit in 1807. But the overthrowal of Napoleon's government was but half the task the Prince of Benevent had set himself, the whole would be accomplished only when he had succeeded in breaking the bonds which he himself had helped to forge between Napoleon and Marie-Louise.

The Emperor believed that whatever misfortunes fate might have in store for him he should always have the supreme consolation afforded by the pleasures of home and the company of his wife and son, and that he had not secured a formal promise from the Empress to rejoin him at Fontainebleau was because he still imagined that her tears might move the Emperor Francis and her future condition be ameliorated. He argued that a certain sovereignty would always be hers by right of birth, that she would be affectionate to him, who would resign himself to the existence of a petty prince, and, believing that she had loved in him rather the man than the sovereign, thought that there might yet be happiness in store for them and for the child whose mental and physical development they would watch over.

Marie-Louise was fond of her husband, disposed to sympathize with his hopes and plans, and willing to rejoin him when the occasion offered, but she was surrounded by people whose influence was all in a contrary direction, and accustomed from childhood to have others think for her, to be guided and ruled, it is not strange that she should have found it hard to follow the dictates of her heart and conscience. The love which she entertained for Napoleon was strong enough to impel her to faithfulness, and it was Talleyrand who took upon himself the task of blighting it. With this object in view he had placed near Marie-Louise a woman who was heart and soul in his schemes, who was naturally an intriguant, and who, whenever she had been able to introduce herself into a diplomatic project, had been quite in her element ; utterly unscrupulous, ignoring the virtue of gratitude, she was precisely the tool whom he required. As lady-in-waiting this woman had ready access to Marie-Louise's ear, and when the other ladies abandoned their posts and returned to their homes Mme. de Brignole remained with the Empress, and, left almost alone with her, seized the occasion to obey Talleyrand's instructions and to instil the poison of doubt into Marie-Louise's mind. Instigated by her master, Mme. de Brignole first insinuated, then affirmed, that Napoleon had never loved his wife, but had constantly deceived her, and when the Empress refused to believe she sent for two valets, who had just abandoned their sovereign and benefactor at Fontainebleau, and had them confirm all her lying tales.

There was no one at hand to inspire with courage and confidence the irresolute young girl who was more wounded by the accounts of her husband's infidelities than prostrated by the fall of her throne; and as she had once allowed herself to be sacrificed, like a modern Iphigenia, so now she acquiesced and stood inertly by, while political expedience sundered the domestic ties, which it had soldered. This compliance was not won in a day, for Marie-Louise struggled nearly a year against overwhelming obstacles, every sentiment was brought into play to alienate her affection from her husband: pride, jealousy, envy, vanity, all were employed, and Bonaparte's enemies triumphed only when they had succeeded in replacing his image in her heart by that of another, when the chaste Emperor of Austria had forced his daughter into a position which publicly compromised her: then monarchal Europe applauded, and the adultress was recompensed by the sovereignty of Parma and Placentia.

Napoleon never dreamt of such abjection; from each of the stopping-places where he rested upon his sad journey he wrote a letter to his wife, as formerly he had written when she was making her triumphal journey towards Paris, greeted by the chiming of bells, the cannon's thunder, and the military salute of imperial marshals. The defeated Emperor, wending his way across Europe under the watchful eyes of the military escort assigned by the allies, with the populace's cries of hatred ringing in his ears, never forgot his wife; but of all the letters which he wrote but two have been published; they are addressed to "My good, my dear Louise." Forgetful of his own sufferings he wrote to her of the pain she must experience, made tender inquiries regarding her health and urged her to be courageous and brave. Care had been taken to inform Napoleon that Marie-Louise's health rendered it imperative that she should take a course of the waters at Aix; it was a means of retarding their reunion and, consciously or not, Corvisart had lent his aid to the Emperor's enemies; but of this, as of all the rest, Napoleon was unsuspicious, and, rejoicing in Corvisart's devotion, he addressed him a letter from Frejus which, if it was merited, is the physician's greatest glory, and far from opposing the journey to Aix the Emperor encouraged it. He thought that though Marie-Louise might not be able to come immediately to Elba, she would surely hasten to install herself at Parma, and, in order that she should miss none of the accessories of rank to which she was accustomed, he dispatched a detachment of Polish light horse to that city to await her arrival and sent a large supply of carriage horses for her use.

Hardly had Napoleon reached Porto-Ferrajo than he began to arrange the Empress's apartments in the palaces destined for his residence, hastening the work with the idea that she might arrive at any hour. He intended to celebrate her coming with fireworks and a grand ball, awaited her arrival to make various excursions to points of interest about the island, and, although foreign to his nature to give public expression to his sentiments, he ordered the painter who was decorating the drawing-room ceiling to depict there "two pigeons fastened together by a slip-knot which tightened as they separated."

It was on Marie-Louise's account that Napoleon kept the visit of Mme. Walewska shrouded in mystery. She had been to Naples to reclaim from Murat the endowment which the Emperor had accorded her from the property which he had reserved, and which Murat had confiscated, and profiting from the relaxed surveillance at Porto-Ferrajo she had solicited an interview with the Emperor.

Bonaparte was then installed at the hermitage of the Madonna de Marciana which was situated in the heart of a forest of aged chestnuts, in whose shade the intense heat of the Corsican summer was more endurable. The Emperor occupied a small house close to the chapel, and the hermits, whom he had not wished to dispossess, were installed in the cellar, while for the accommodation of his suite which consisted of a captain of mounted police, named Paoli-Bernotti, an officer of ordinance, several Mamalukes and two *valets de chambre,* Marchand and Saint Denis, a large tent had been erected under the chestnut trees and close to a little spring which lost itself in a carpet of fresh moss besprinkled with wild lilies of the valley and violets. Dinner was never served at the hermitage, the Emperor descending every evening to Marciana and dining with his mother, who was installed there.

On the receipt of Mme. Walewska's letter the Emperor at once prepared for her visit, but the orders regarding the arrangements for her reception were so given that the name of the expected guest was kept a profound secret. She disembarked at Porto-Ferrajo during the night of September 1st, and found awaiting her on the quay a carriage and four, and three saddled horses in charge of Bernotti. Accompanied by her sister and little son she entered the carriage, while her brother, Colonel Laczinski, mounted one of the horses, and in the bright moonlight they set off for Marciana. The Emperor, accompanied by Paoli and two Mamalukes awaited their coming at Procchio, and there Mme. Walewska was also obliged to mount one of the horses as it was impossible for the carriage to go further; Bernotti took charge of the little boy and the party finally arrived at the summit of the mountain. Dismounting before the hermitage the Emperor assisted Mme. Walewska from her saddle, and, hat in hand pointed to the house saying: "Madame, there is my palace to which you are heartily welcome;" and abandoning the house to the ladies he himself went to sleep in the tent which sheltered his suite and servants.

The close of the night was stormy, and in the early morning the Emperor, who had been unable to sleep, called Marchand and questioned him as to whether any gossip had been caused by the arrival of his visitors; he was informed by the valet that it was rumored in Porto-Ferrajo that the mysterious lady was none other than the Empress, and the child the little King of Rome, and that, moved by this rumor, Doctor Foureau had hastened to the hermitage to offer his services and was at that moment awaiting the Emperor's command.

Napoleon dressed and left the tent. The morning was bright and beautiful with no trace of the furious storm of the previous night, and on the mountain side in the bright sunshine, the mysterious child was playing happily. The Emperor called the boy and seating himself in a chair which Marchand brought, took him upon his knee; he then sent the valet in search of Dr. Foureau and when the latter appeared said, pointing to the child: "Well, Foureau, what do you think of him?" "Sire," responded the Doctor, "the king has grown tremendously," at which answer Napoleon laughed heartily, for young Walewski was a year older than the King of Rome, but his beautiful features and the blond curls which fell in profusion over his shoulders caused him to resemble his half-brother closely, or rather, to resemble Isabey's popular portrait of the King of Rome.

Napoleon chatted for some moments with the physician, then, thanking him for the friendship manifested by the prompt offer of his services, dismissed him and turned to greet Mme. Walewska whom he espied about leaving the hermitage. Breakfast, which had been ordered from Marciana, was served under the chestnut trees; the meal passed off gaily, and the rest of the day was spent by the Emperor and Mme. Walewska in walking and talking together.

At dinner the Emperor desired that the boy, of whom he had seen but little during the day, should sit at his side, and when Mme. Walewska objected on the score of the child's boisterous ways he insisted, saying that he did not mind the child's roguishness, his own childhood having been a turbulent one. When they were seated at table the Emperor recounted anecdotes of his boyhood telling how he used to beat his brother Joseph and force him to do his bidding, and how his mother had punished him by giving him only dry bread to eat—bread which he had given to the shepherd boys in exchange for their chestnut bread, or else thrown away and gone to his foster-mother's where he was fed on the best the house afforded and caressed to his heart's content. Young Walewska, who had at first been overawed by the presence of so many grown people at table and had behaved in most exemplary manner, was emboldened by the Emperor's stories to give vent to his naturally high spirits, whereupon Napoleon said:

"I see, my lad, that you don't fear the whip. . . . well I advise you to! I never got a beating but once, but I've never forgotten it." He then went on to relate how Pauline and himself had once made sport of their mother and been soundly whipped by her in consequence. The boy listened attentively, and when the Emperor had finished speaking exclaimed with an air of conviction: "I shall never be whipped for *that*, I would not make fun of *my* mother," whereupon the Emperor embraced him tenderly saying, "That was well said."

At eight o'clock that evening the visitors returned to Ponte-Ferrajo, and re-embarked for Naples; in indemnification for the confiscations of Murat, Mme. Walewska carried with her a draft on the Emperor's treasurer for sixty-one thousand francs. It is said that her stay at Naples was so prolonged, that March of 1815 still found her there.

In spite of all the precautions taken to keep Mme. Walewska's visit to Elba a secret, it became known, for there were too many people interested in the Emperor's movements, too many spies about him, to keep such a visit from being talked of. The islanders insisted that the mysterious lady was Marie-Louise, but the English and Bourbon spies were better informed, and their employers believed that this visit heralded the renewal of the Emperor's relations with the Polish woman. In reality, Mme. Walewska's journey to Elba was actuated rather by friendship and sympathy than by love, and the presence of her sister, Mlle. Laczinska, at the Hermitage, proves that the visit was a conventional one.

If Napoleon had any love-affair while at Elba, it certainly was not with the so-called Countess de Rohan, who was but a vulgar adventuress, and went to the island to reclaim no one knows what, from the Emperor, and to offer him her company in his exile, but rather with a woman who has been much less discussed ; the same whom he had received several times in his apartments in the orangery, at Saint-Cloud, and who, unsolicited, repaired to Ponte-Ferrajo. Whether this lady was married to Colonel B * * * * when she went to Elba, or married him there is not known, but, wed or not, her devotion to the fallen Emperor was great, and it is unfortunate that so little is known regarding the details of her life. What we do know is, that, not content with having followed Napoleon to Elba, she went to Rambouillet in 1815 and besought his permission to follow him to St. Helena, that she was heart-broken at his refusal, and that with three thousand francs which were given her, she went to the United States, where she hoped to find him.

Little attention seems to have been attracted by Napoleon's intimacy with this woman, while certain letters, written by a miserable priest in the pay of the Duke de Blacas, have been republished periodically ; these letters were written with the view of accrediting calumnious reports which were then afloat, and it is needless to dwell upon them here.

While at Elba, Napoleon passed through a moral and political crisis which rendered the greatest reserve obligatory ; he knew that the slightest indiscretion would be related to Marie-Louise, and enlarged upon by his enemies who surrounded her, and that she would be deeply wounded thereby. He had sent Captain Hurault de Sorbée, the husband of one of her ladies, to Aix-les-Bains, with instructions to essay to speak with the Empress, and deliver his messages in person, and had received news which led him to hope that a regular correspondence would soon be established between them; thus it was scarcely the moment to become entangled in a scandalous intrigue. Time passed, the month of September dragged its weary length along without bringing the Emperor a word from his wife or son, and at length, worn out by anxiety and unfulfilled hope, he determined to write to the Duke of Tuscany, upon whose friendship he still relied and whom he had designated to his wife as their natural intermediary. The letter he sent the duke was not supplicatory, from the manner in which he addressed, as "My dear brother and uncle;" it is evident that Napoleon remembered the favors his highness had received at his hands, and believed that the one-time parasite of Compiègne must also bear them in mind. "Having received no news of my wife since August 10th, nor of my son in six months," he writes, "I beg your royal highness to inform me if you will permit me to send weekly letters to my wife in your care, whether you will undertake to keep me informed regarding her health, etc., and to forward letters from my son's governess, Mme. de Montesquiou. I flatter myself that, in spite of the events which have changed so many persons, your highness still entertains some friendship for me ; if you assure me of this by granting my request, it will be a great consolation and comfort, and, in that case, I beg your highness to show yourself favorably disposed towards this little canton which shares the loyal sentiments of Tuscany for your person. I trust your highness does not doubt the sincerity of the sentiments I have always expressed, nor my esteem and regard ; and I beg to be kindly remembered to your highness's children."

It was simply a question of a friendly service to be rendered one who confessed himself unhappy and admitted himself defeated, and who, to soften the prince's heart, almost avowed himself his subject, yet it was not a supplication, and the old equality, nay, superiority of rank, pierces through the carefully-worded lines. There was no answer to this letter, for the drama was ended, the imperial house of Austria had succeeded in dishonoring its daughter, and the Empress of France had fallen so low as to become the mistress of her own chamberlain.

After such a letter, written to such a man, Napoleon would not take any further action ; his wife and child had been stolen from him, the Bourbons no longer paid the annual sum stipulated for at Fontainebleau, and he saw that he should be forced to disband his guard, and, unable to offer even a semblance of resistance, be killed with his faithful followers, should the allied sovereigns order his transportation to some remote island, the Azores for example, as Talleyrand had suggested on the 13th of October, because, as he then said : "They were five hundred miles from any land."

The Emperor foresaw that he must either submit to being transported by the sovereigns, or assassinated by the bandits in Brulart's pay ; and preferring to make a supreme effort and risk all for France, determined upon his return.

CHAPTER XIX.

THE HUNDRED DAYS.

On New Year's day, 1815, Napoleon had received a letter from the Empress, giving him news of their son, telling what a handsome and charming child he was, and that he would soon be able to write himself to his father. It is impossible to say why this letter was written, possibly it was prompted by remorse, but whatever actuated Marie-Louise it served to strengthen the tie between herself and Napoleon, and confirmed his conviction that she had never abandoned the intention of rejoining him, that her silence was compulsory, and that, were she free to do so, she would hasten to his side.

He was convinced that, had he a throne to offer, Marie-Louise's jailors would set her at liberty, and as soon as he felt assured of the success of his enterprise he hastened to inform her, writing from Lyons on the 12th of March. Marie-Louise, however, did with this letter, as she had done with all those she had received from Elba, handed it over to her father who communicated its contents to the allied plenipotentiaries, and Napoleon received no answer.

Immediately upon re-entering Paris the Emperor ordered that the Empress's apartments should be put in order and re-established her household upon its old footing. Ten days later, upon the 1st of April, he wrote an official letter to the Austrian Emperor wherein he reclaimed the "objects of my tenderest affection, my wife and son." "As," he wrote, "the long separation necessitated by circumstances has caused me the greatest sorrow I have ever experienced, I desire that my wife and child be speedily restored to me, and am assured that our reunion is as earnestly desired by the virtuous princess, whose destiny Your Majesty united with mine, as by myself;" and he terminated the letter by saying: "I know too well Your Majesty's principles and the value Your Highness places upon family-ties not to feel assured that, despite the disposition of your cabinet, or questions of political expediency, Your Majesty will accelerate the reunion of a wife with her husband, a son with his father."

Like the others this letter remained unanswered, and the obstinate silence, opposed alike to official and family letters, confirmed Napoleon's belief that it was the political attitude of the house of Austria and the pressure brought to bear upon her which paralyzed the natural desire of his wife and prevented her rejoining him, he therefore determined to employ secret means for communicating with her. With this object he sent to Vienna carefully chosen messengers, Flahaut and Montrond, men who could be trusted and who possessed facilities for approaching Marie-Louise. Montrond alone pierced the lines, but when he was about to give to the Empress the letter of which he was the bearer, Meneval interposed. The ci-devant secretary of Napoleon, who had become, in 1813, the Empress's secretary and had followed her to Austria, understood only too well the relations existing between his royal mistress and Count Neipperg, and he felt that in burning the Emperor's tender letter which he had written to his wife, he was rendering him a service. Nevertheless, Meneval dared not write directly to Napoleon informing him of the real state of affairs, for he realized what a terrible blow it would be to his master, and he therefore determined to inform one in whose unwavering fidelity he had implicit confidence of the *liaison*, and wrote an anonymous letter to Lavallette; Count de Lavallette, however, saw in this anonymous communication only a political machination, and it is not strange that Napoleon shared his views.

They were soon to be enlightened, however, for

Ballouhey, secretary of expenses for the two Empresses and a man whose fidelity and honesty were unquestionable, was *en route* from Vienna by way of Munich, where he was to receive some instructions from Prince Eugène. The Emperor was so impatient to see Ballouhey that he ordered his arrival at Belfort to be telegraphed him, and stationed an orderly at his house in Paris with instructions to conduct the secretary to the Elysée the instant he appeared.

Ballouhey reached Paris on the 28th of April and was closeted for two hours with the Emperor, but, though Napoleon received a clear and concise statement of Prince Eugène's ideas of the political situation, he failed to obtain definite information upon the subject nearest his heart. Ballouhey was a scrupulously exact accountant; he had been deeply attached both to Josephine and Marie-Louise; but he was a timorous man and dared not affirm the truth of the scandalous *liaison* which was an open secret in Vienna.

Meneval, expelled from Vienna, arrived a fortnight later, and from him the whole truth was learned. On taking leave of the Empress she had charged him to say to his imperial master "that, while she would take no step towards securing a divorce, she believed he would offer no objection to an amicable separation." "Such a separation," she said, "was indispensable, but it would not impair the sentiments of esteem and gratitude which she entertained for him," and she added that " her decision to remain apart from Napoleon was irrevocable, and not even her father had the right to oblige her to return to France." It was Marie-Louise who, putting herself under the protection of the allied plenipotentiaries in an official letter dated March 12th, provoked the furious declaration which was signed by them on the 13th, and in recompense for her act Count Neipperg was created court chamberlain; and it was with her consent that, on the 18th of March, the little King of Rome was separated from his governess, Mme. de Montesquiou, and deprived of all his French servants.

Undoubtedly, Meneval added other, and more private details, for it was no longer right to conceal the monstrous truth; possibly Marie-Louise was then in the early stages of one of those pregnancies which were to people the avenues of Burg with adulterous bastards, entitled princes and highnesses to the everlasting shame of the royal house of Austria.

When, after the birth of the King of Rome, Dubois, the *accoucheur*, affirmed that a second child would imperil Marie-Louise's life, Napoleon, despite his desire for numerous offspring and a second son to sit on the throne of Italy, had bowed to the physician's decision : M. de Neipperg had no such scruples and proved repeatedly that Baron Dubois had been mistaken. Although the Emperor could no longer doubt the unfaithfulness of Marie-Louise, it was necessary to keep the truth from the nation and essential that the people should conserve their illusions regarding their Empress; twelve months previous he considered that nothing would appeal more to the people than the thought of that woman and child confided to France; to-day the captivity in which they were held, the separation which violated all laws, human and divine, the attempted violation of conjugal faith and paternal love committed by the sovereigns in arms for the re-establishment in France of a government like their own, seemed to him of a nature to appeal to every generous and honest instinct in the heart of men and patriots. The grief which the Empress felt when she was torn from the post which it was her duty to fill, the thirty sleepless nights which she had passed in 1814, the real imprisonment to which she had been subjected, the treaty of Fontainebleau, violated by the kings who had torn from him his wife and son, the indignant cry of the old Queen Marie-Caroline to her granddaughter:

"Since you are prohibited from going out by the door, escape by the window and fly to rejoin your husband," the King of Rome—then called the Prince Imperial—separated from his mother, Mme. de Montesquiou driven away and trembling for her pupil's life, the Emperor wished Meneval to recount it all and ordered a report to be prepared in case the Chamber made a motion for the King of Rome. The Chamber!

Not once during the hundred days, not once during the six years of agony at Saint Helena, did a word of censure or bitterness against Marie-Louise escape him; he invariably spoke of her with affection and kindly pity; he thought of her only as she was when she first came to France, young, fresh, loyal and unsullied; there is not one of his companions in captivity who has not reported his conversations regarding her almost in the same terms. If a European ship dropped anchor in Jamestown Bay Napoleon was sure that he was about to receive a letter from the Empress, and nervous, anxious and unable to work, would pass the whole day in expectancy; when one of his servants was taken from him his first thought was to send a letter by that sure hand to Marie-Louise, as for example the one he confided to his surgeon in which he said: "Should the bearer of this see you, my good Louise, I beg of you to permit him to kiss your hands." In his will, which was dated the 5th of April, 1821, he wrote this phrase: "I never have had any fault to find with my dear wife, the Empress Marie-Louise; to my last moment I shall retain for her the most tender sentiments, and I beg her to watch over my son and guard against the dangers which still surround his childhood;" and, as if this was not enough, he bequeathed to her from the modest wardrobe which now constituted his sole fortune, all his laces, and on the 28th of April, a week before his death, he instructed Antommarchi to take his heart from his body and send it to her. "Preserve my heart in alcohol," he said to the physician, "and take it yourself to Parma to my dear Marie-Louise; tell her that I love her tenderly and have never ceased to love her, recount to her all that you have seen, all that touches my situation and my death."

Truly Hudson Lowe did well in obliging Antommarchi to place the silver vase which contained Napoleon's heart in his coffin: What would Count Neipperg have done with it?

In default of the perfidious Austrian, many other women, from France, Ireland and Poland surrounded the Emperor during the last glorious days of his short reign of three months, encouraging his spirit by their enthusiasm and devotion, pleasing his eye by their beauty; while even those who were least fitted for political intrigues became his spies and informants, and by instinct rather than reason, frequently gave counsel which might well have been followed; for example, George regarding Fouché; Mme. Pellapra who hastened to return to Paris from Lyons and warned him of the Duke d'Otrante's intentions, and Mme. Walewska, who, hastily returning from Naples, was immediately received with her son at the Elysée, brought messages from Murat. Mme. * * * * was among the first to present herself to the Emperor, and assuming her title and rank as lady of the palace, was among the faithful ones of the 20th of March, and among those who, in the brilliantly illuminated salon of the Tuileries, impatiently awaited the arrival of the exile of Elba. There were many others, Mme. Dulauloy, Mme. Lavallette, Mme. Ney, Mme. Regnauld de Saint-Jean-d'Angely, Mme. de Beauvau and Mme. de Turenne, all of whom vied with each other in the endeavor to encourage and please him. At that time there breathed upon these women of France that divine afflatus which creates heroines and martyrs, inspires acts of supreme devotion and courage, and strengthens souls to face courageously the severest trials.

During that sinister period, which is justly called,

"the White Terror," a period of atrocities which to-day we vainly seek to palliate, the women of the Empire manifested, amidst the universal cowardliness of mankind, a courage, energy and presence of mind which immortalizes them; at the Tuileries during the hundred days, at Malmaison and after Waterloo, they proved how well they knew how to show their loyalty and honor misfortune.

It was not alone the well known and the celebrated, but the humble and the obscure who showed their devotion; as, for example, a woman, who, at the review of the confederation, approached the Emperor and handed him a petition, a roll of paper carefully fastened, from which, when it was opened, there fell twenty-five bank notes of a thousand francs each; and another who, on the 23d of June, the eve of the day upon which Napoleon was to leave the Elysée for Malmaison, wrote to his *valet de chambre*, requesting him to meet her at the church of Saint-Philippe du Roule to receive an important communication. Marchand went to the rendezvous, and found at the place indicated a woman engaged in prayer; she was veiled, but not heavily enough to hide her features, which were exceptionally beautiful; Marchand approached and asked in what way he could serve her. The mysterious lady hesitated for a moment, then, with extreme embarrassment, replied that the misfortunes of the Emperor had touched her deeply, that she wished to see, to console and love him. Napoleon, on hearing of her desire, smiled and said : " Hers is an admiration which might lead to an intrigue ; it must not be encouraged," but the naïve offer of this heart, coming on such a day and at such an hour, touched him profoundly, and later, upon several occasions, he spoke of the mysterious lady of Saint-Philippe du Roule.

Did he find in captivity some woman who gave to him the consolation which only a tender woman can give to a man ? We know about his childish romps with Miss Elizabeth Balcombe, during her sojourn at Briars ; and we divine a familiarity with a woman whose conduct during the Empire would seemingly have forbidden her to approach him, and who, twice divorced, dismissed from court, had, by the simple fact of his marriage, brought disgrace upon her third husband. But if the testamentary liberality which the Emperor showed this person gives some weight to the reports of the foreign Commissioners, if her presence really occasioned discord among the Emperor's companions, and her departure was one of the painful experiences which he was obliged to live through, one yet knows too little regarding this portion of the drama of Saint

Helena to expatiate upon it; the woman plied her rôle upon the island; that is all that one can say.

Side by side with this retired courtesan, whom interest had taken to Rochefort, and whom interest retained at Saint Helena, we find another woman, who is really worthy of admiration. By birth and by her relationship with the Fitz-James family, Countess Bertrand was entitled to one of the best positions at Court, and, had she remained in Paris, would doubtless have been one of the leaders of society, but she voluntarily shared her husband's devotion to his chief and followed him into exile; she lived in a cabin infested with rats, within reach of the Emperor, but unable to succor or amuse him. She remained until the end, compassionate, sensible and dignified, guarding her honor like a Roman matron, and like a statue of grief she followed the procession which conducted the captive conqueror to his grave in the valley of Géranium, and she, an Englishwoman by birth, was the only woman who wept over the remains of him whom her countrymen had murdered.

CHAPTER XX.

SUMMARY.

The sum of the preceding chapters only signified that Napoleon was subject to the same desires, passions and weaknesses as other men, and had taken no vows of continence; that the amorous side of his nature was twofold, on one side the physical alone reigned, on the other physical and moral united ... the moral being in the ascendant.

We have hidden none of the adventures wherein the animal part of his nature alone predominated; not because one can glean from them a special insight into his character, but because to hide them would give rise to the suspicion that they were wholly unfavorable to his general character. Because he was NAPOLEON all that he did was known, and no matter how carefully he hid his amorous intrigues they were sure to be discovered; ladies-in-waiting and ladies'-maids, aides-de-camp and valets were ceaselessly on the watch, and no matter how insignificant the events which transpired they were all carefully noted. Everybody at the Tuileries lived in the governmental zone, whether they were soliciting favors or hunting for news, and all took a lively interest in the doings of the Emperor, and each made a note of any incident which came under his observation. As everything, Napoleon did, has an historical interest, as his lightest words, slightest actions, even the trifling ailments which from time to time afflicted him, have been of interest to the public for a hundred years, and as many erroneous tales have been accredited, the sole course for the author of this book to pursue is to establish facts, and relate such adventures as are authenticated by the according narrations of various reliable persons; if any have been omitted, or simply referred to, it is because they have been related by but one chronicler and it has been impossible to discover documentary proof of their authenticity, or sometimes because they were of so commonplace a nature as to render it useless to dwell upon them.

There were women always ready to gratify his desires, whether expressed by himself or made known by his messengers; he accepted their willingly-given caresses, sometimes from physical necessity, sometimes from voluptuousness; but he never experienced mental exhaustion or fatigue from his adventures, nor did any woman distract him from his work; of all these women none was seduced by him, for if there was a virgin among their number she was one who trafficked on her virtue.

In order to judge the men of the Empire, above all, Napoleon, by the narrow and hypocritical standard of contemporaneous times one must place them in similar environments; their lives were not the humdrum, monotonous lives of the modern business man, they were always in the saddle, death on the crupper, galloping from one end of Europe to the other amidst a rain of bullets, and if some of them, unknown to the Emperor, trailed their mistresses after them, the majority gave little thought to the senses and remained chaste during the campaigns.

If, on their return from a long war, or when a city was conquered and there was a lull in the strife, brute passion gained the mastery, does it signify that they were the most debauched of mankind? To have followed the calling which they selected from preference and clung to from ambition must they not have been, by origin and nature, stronger, more brutal, more like the primitive man, than the men of this generation? Did not their profession develop, accentuate and foster all that was savage, combative and animal in their natures? Had they not the same tastes, desires and appetites as other men ? Was it to be expected that they would remain scrupulously faithful to wives whom they rarely saw ?

Some few, indeed, were faithful, and there are admirable examples of fidelity, tenderness and delicacy given by those men of war, but for the majority the distractions of the camp and garrison intrigues were the rule, and they placed no importance upon them.

Side by side with these animal appetites they entertained ingenuously sentimental ideas of conjugal tenderness, and nothing was too good or too precious for the wife who had almost invariably been married for love and from the most disinterested motives ; to satisfy her tastes they pillaged Europe, throwing their spoils at her feet ; to content her caprices and ambitions they deployed an amount of patience and diplomacy which would make one smile were it not so touching.

In generosity, in the care for his wife, in letters, presents, and in the wealth showered upon her, Napoleon was not outdone by any of his warriors, but his sentimentalism was of another origin and essence than theirs.

The soldiers of the Empire, who had neither by nature nor by education any scruples, fabricated a code of honor for themselves, and although they fondly believed the sword had made them the equals of the men of gentle birth whose places they had usurped, and whom they hated, their "soldier's code" differed in many respects from that attributed by Montesquieu to gentlemen; but in their days they could hardly search for the rules regulating that code of honor, and they did not care to take a Lauzun or a Tilly for their model; they still detested those whom they had replaced, and if they laid claim to the title of "gentlemen" it was because they considered themselves the equals of men of noble ancestry.

From 1806 everything in France was modeled on the troubadour style, novels, historical works, pictures, dress and drama, but it was less a question of the troubadour himself, than of him of whom he sang; the knight who professed the adoration of his lady, who for his exploits in the Holy Land received a scarf embroidered by her fair hands and considered his deeds of valor well rewarded by a glance from her dear eyes. The warriors of the Empire made every effort to model themselves after these ideal chevaliers, and though they did not gird themselves with the fair one's colors, many a man wore a sword-knot embroidered by her, or wore the beloved one's portrait over his heart, and decorated himself with some bauble of her giving upon state occasions.

Napoleon yielded less to this current than his followers, than Prince Eugène and certain of his marshals, but the ambient atmosphere finally affected him also, as certain incidents in his relations with Marie-Louise prove conclusively; but it was not, however, until the close of the Empire that a sentiment, until then unexperienced, awoke in him and effaced all others.

Up to that time Napoleon's sentimentalism was in no degree influenced by the literature of the time, but greatly by that of a previous era. Rousseau had influenced him, as his letters to Josephine, Mme. * * * * and Mme. Walewska show; in all of them may be found the same tone, the identical expressions and words which were used by the young Lieutenant Bonaparte when from Valence he complained of his loneliness and poverty.

A pupil of Jean-Jacques, Napoleon was so thoroughly impregnated with the ideas of his master, that he, who had striven for and obtained, even the impossible, in the order of events, encountered only impotence, negation and disgust in the range of sentiments. In Napoleon's continual search for a woman who would love him for himself, whose only thought would be for him, who would live but for him, and with whom he could dwell in a constant interchange of tenderness, he certainly acted in good faith ; but who can tell up to what point he was influenced by his literary souvenirs, or how much he forced himself in the effort to experience sensations which he believed to be rare and strange.

That which gives us reason to think that he forced his nature is that he soon wearied ; he received less pleasure than he anticipated in the society of the woman he wooed, and the real woman seemed invariably inferior to the ideal creature of his imagination ; the sentimentalism which was cultivated found itself in opposition to the positivism which was natural, and he ruptured the much-sought-for relations ; but only to run in search of a new sensation, a fresh experience, as soon as the occasion offered.

In such a man his fidelity, not of the senses, but of the heart, is surprising ; he had mistresses whom he loved sincerely, and he divorced Josephine, yet she held a place apart in his heart and he ever felt a deep and tender affection for her, an affection so strong that he pardoned all her faults and the wrongs she had done him ; nay, more, he forgot them.

Josephine's life, of which he did not fail to keep himself informed, must have revolted him, but he shut his eyes to it, and remembered only that the woman whom he had raised to be the first lady in France, who was associated with his destiny, was grace itself and elegance personified; he endowed her with all the virtues and graces which a passionate lover showers upon his mistress, and, although he reproached her for her prodigality, he proved his affection by giving her the means to gratify all her desires.

To the end of his days Napoleon ignored the true Josephine, and threw over the love of his youth a halo of imaginary charms and virtues which has immortalized her; if he thus deceived posterity it was because he was himself deceived, and to the very end he persisted in the illusions, holding before his eyes, in his heart and senses, at Saint Helena, the Josephine whom he had seen for the first time in the rue Chantereine, the woman in whose arms he first tasted the sweets of love.

Napoleon's love for Josephine was such as a man gives to his mistress, a love without respect, which puts no restraint upon itself, exacts instant satisfaction and does not fear disagreements; which voluntarily confesses its infidelities and relates *risquée* anecdotes; that such was Napoleon's affection for Josephine is proved by the fact that at each evolution of his destiny he realized more forcibly that his interests demanded he should break with her and rupture the union which was not a marriage in his eyes because it had not for eight years been sanctioned by the Church, and because, when it did receive the Church's blessing, he had appeared before the priest by force. Had Josephine given him a child he would have considered the contract valid, but, being childless, he considered himself free, and when he separated himself from her he treated her like a mistress, consoling her by large sums of money and arranging for her existence in an opulent style.

One may question whether, in spite of the weakness Napoleon had for Josephine, despite his showering favors and presents upon her, adopting her children and elevating her relatives to posts of honor, Napoleon ever regarded her as of his family; so great was the difference between the sentiments he entertained for her and those inspired by Marie-Louise, particularly after Marie-Louise had borne him a child. Then the conjugal spirit took possession of and dominated him; undoubtedly he never gave her the passionate love he had bestowed upon his first wife, but he entertained for Marie-Louise a respect which he never gave to Josephine. While he had invariably refused all participation in affairs of state to his first wife he voluntarily accorded it to the second, discovering in her greater intelligence than he accorded to his oldest councillors or even to his brothers. With Josephine the sentimental side of his nature as developed by Rousseau was dominant, while with Marie-Louise his Corsican atavism and the traditions of his native mountains resumed their supremacy: Marie-Louise was sanctified in his view by her motherhood.

Napoleon would never admit that his wife had abandoned him and deceived him; she was his wife, the mother of his son, and that placed her above the temptations and weakness common to her sex. So dominant was the conjugal spirit in him that, to the hour of his death, he ignored her treachery, and that he, who was so jealous of the woman he had once possessed that he complained bitterly of Mme. Walewska's marriage, never uttered a complaint against his wife. Was his silence occasioned by the desire of securing for her the respect which a monarchal lord requires paid to crowned heads, did it make him happier to ignore her faults, did he find excuses for them in the extraordinary circumstances surrounding her, or did he hope that the secret he refused to reveal would be better guarded by history? Possibly he was actuated by all these motives, but his predominant thought was, that she was his wife, and therefore could not fall.

Thus, separating the purely sensual *liaisons*, which were brief, from the deep attachments of his life, we find in Napoleon as great a faculty for love as for thought and action, and are obliged to admit that he was as astonishing a husband as he was a warrior and a statesman.

There remains but one point to be considered, whether any of the women with whom Napoleon was closely related ever swayed him sufficiently to affect his political views and moves; it does not appear that any woman, either wife or mistress, directly influenced him, but doubtless the impressions received from both, the ideas they advanced and the circumstances accompanying certain of his *liaisons* gave rise to new ideas in his brain and modified old ones.

Dearly loved as Josephine was, she was not among those who were the primary cause of certain political moves. It has been affirmed that it was her influence which surrounded him with people of noble birth and led him, at times, to sacrifice the spirit of the revolution to the traditions of the old *régime*, but that is an error; Josephine sought to draw the old nobility round Napoleon by his order, and it was at his command that she protected them. An insight into the various gradations of society under the old *régime*, some false impressions, some information, much of which was inexact, was about all he gleaned from her. The birth of a son to Mlle. Denuelle de la Plaegne doubtless first determined him to divorce Josephine, and that of Mme. Walewska's cemented his resolution, while his political attitude towards Poland is explained if one remembers who was his mistress and close companion from 1807 to 1809, even his long friendship for Bernadotte becomes comprehensible when one recalls his tenderness for Désirée.

When Napoleon married Marie-Louise and became, through her, a member of the house of Austria, he believed the relationship so formed was close and binding, as the tie which bound him to his own family, and his faith in the Austrian Emperor's friendship, his confidence in his wife's fidelity and discretion is due to his belief in the strength and indestructibility of ties of blood and his conviction that they alone rendered a political alliance inviolate. Marie-Louise, not because she was unusually intelligent, but because of the rôle she played in his political combinations and the prestige of her motherhood, exercised an unprecedented influence over him. Napoleon set a high value upon ties of blood and the obligations entailed by kinship; he was a true Corsican in the strength of his attachment and his adherence to family, and it appears as if the very value he placed upon the ties which should be the strongest and most sacred to humanity caused his fall.

If women had played no rôle in his life, Napoleon would cease to be the amazing example of masculine genius that he is, and would become a sexless being without interest to humanity because not subject to the failings and passions of other men, uninfluenced by the traditions which sway them, possessed of no sentiment common to mankind. As it was, this man, whose genius was astounding, who, served by an unparalleled fortune, accomplished the greatest task that mortal ever undertook, was precisely the man to whom no emotion was a stranger.

It is human to be influenced by, to believe in and to love woman, to experience by her and for her all the sensations and emotions which she inspires, and in that respect, as in all others, Napoleon was superior to mankind.

THE END.

www.ingramcontent.com/pod-product-compliance
Lightning Source LLC
Chambersburg PA
CBHW030003240426
43672CB00007B/804